A Russian Childhood

A Russian Childhood

E. N. VODOVOSOVA

translated by
ANTHONY BRODE AND
OLGA LANE

FABER AND FABER
24 Russell Square
London

*First published in mcmlxi
by Faber and Faber Limited
24 Russell Square London W.C.1
Printed in Great Britain by
Latimer Trend & Co Ltd Plymouth*

Contents

I

Living Above Our Means

My parents' country estate was different from those of our neighbours, and so was the kind of life we lived. 'Are you going to be at the Tsevlovskys'?' one neighbour would ask another; and the reply would be 'Yes, of course—they're doing a new comedy and the whole family's going over to see it.'

From miles around visitors would come to our estate, which was called Pogoreloye—not only the members of the landowning families but all their retainers including governesses, valets and maids. All would stay at Pogoreloye and during 'theatre days' both house and outbuildings were full of people.

Theatres in those days were very rare even in towns, and quite undreamed of in the country. My father had started an amateur theatre, though not for his own amusement: 'It will be very valuable for the children,' he used to say whenever Mother complained that the whole idea was far too expensive. But though her complaints were not unreasonable—for a large family like ours with so many children, the theatre and the constant hospitality it involved were more than we could afford—Father was right, too: for my brothers and sisters (I was too small to take part in the acting) the theatre was of great importance.

Many landowners envied my parents their theatre and their

happy affectionate family, and as they left Pogoreloye the gossip would go: 'They live far above their means, you know. Just think how much the theatre and the entertaining must cost them! And those serfs acting and singing and playing the violin when they should be working. It's not right, really it isn't.'

It is perfectly true that the theatre and the entertaining cost a lot of money; so much that after a few years on his estate Father began to realize the necessity of establishing his affairs on a better footing. Before long he was offered the post of district judge in a small town called Porechye, accepted, and moved there with all the family. It delighted him to think that we should have to listen no longer to conversations about how cleverly one landowner had diddled his friend over the sale of a horse, or how another thrashed all the peasants in the village, from ancient grandfather to five-year-old grand-daughter, because one of them had committed some mis-demeanour.

Father did not abandon the theatre in town—on the contrary, it was easier to maintain there. He sent for comedies by Fonvizin and Griboyedov and we acted them at our new home, which consisted of a large wooden house with many outbuildings and a beautiful garden. One of the outbuildings Father requisitioned for the theatre and, as before, visitors used to come long distances for the performances. The expenses remained the same.

It was quite obvious to Mother that Father was approaching bankruptcy; but when she compared her children with those of her neighbours she took note of our conversations and our interests and decided as a result not to argue with her husband. Our life continued therefore just as before except that we spent each winter in the town and left each spring for the country. Our estate supplied us with food and linen and leather and we were dressed from head to foot by the serfs:

and so we continued to live in a grand style without a care in the world.

There was one person who was just as close and dear to us as our parents: our nurse Masha, who had special reasons for her devotion to the family and remembered Father's kindness to her as long as she lived.

She had had a very unhappy childhood: her father kept a country inn and made his wife and daughter work like slaves. His temper was very quick and the slightest mistake was an excuse for cruelty. When Masha was fourteen her mother died; she found it difficult to manage the house and was often beaten by her father. After six months she found out that her father was going to marry again—and marry a very bad-tempered woman at that. Realizing that she could not face life with a stepmother, she decided that the only thing she could do was run away.

One spring day as Masha came out on to the steps of the house a group of wandering beggars went past and stopped for a rest near by. Their songs and tales sounded so fascinating that she made up her mind to join them.

So Masha became a beggar; but soon she found the nomadic existence in all weathers, the nights spent on bare ground and the rough ways and dishonesty of the beggars were even worse than her life at home, so she left them and wandered around on her own begging for her bread. One day Father, travelling on business, happened to find her lying unconscious at the side of the road: pale and thin in her torn and dirty dress, her feet scratched and filthy, she had obviously collapsed from cold and hunger. Father picked her up and took her to a hospital.

Before he left for home a few days later, Father visited Masha and gave her some money and the address of our estate—promising her that if ever she made her way there she would be looked after. When she recovered Masha lived a long time going from one house to another doing heavy work to earn her living: what she earned was only enough to keep a roof over her head. Eventually she found a place as nurse in the house of a rich merchant, where she spent over five years. She decided to save enough money to start the long journey to her benefactor; and that was how she appeared in our family, with tired face and black circles round her eyes and deep lines by her mouth.

From then on Masha lived with us and became nurse to us children. In spite of the fact that she was not our serf she considered herself out of gratitude the slave of my parents and of each member of the family.

In the spring of 1848 there was an outbreak of cholera in the town and we made ready to leave for the country earlier than usual. Every day there was news of somebody dead or sick, but nobody imagined that tragedy might be knocking at our door.

One night not long before our departure my sister Sasha woke up and called for Nanny, but there was no answer. Sasha lit a candle and saw that she was not in the room—her bed hadn't even been slept in. She was so frightened that she woke her brothers and sisters and we stared at her empty bed in amazement, wondering why she had never got into it.

'Quiet, quiet!' hissed Sasha suddenly. 'Listen!'

For a moment the room was silent and then we heard a noise—the running of feet and some kind of disturbance on the other side of the wall. Then Sasha jumped out of bed, threw the door open wide, and began to call loudly for Nanny.

We realized that something was wrong the instant she ran into the room. Her hands were trembling, and tears were pouring down her face; she looked at us in bewilderment without saying anything. We jumped out of bed and ran to her, throwing our arms round her.

'Nanny, darling! What's the matter, why are you crying?'

'Daddy is ill . . . your daddy. . . .' Her voice was shaking and tears ran down her wrinkled cheeks. 'Pray to God to have pity on you and not let you become orphans.' With these words she fell on her knees before the icons; barefooted, clad only in our night-shirts, we knelt also, and at that moment Mother's voice could be heard from the corridor calling Nanny.

Every hour Father grew worse; during the day the doctor called several times, but obviously had no hope he might improve. Watching through the keyhole, we saw him gesticulate helplessly and shake his head.

When Nanny brought us our dinner her hands were trembling so much that she couldn't dish it up, and she lowered herself on to a chair and asked my sister Sasha to do it for her.

In the evening Father felt a little better and fell into a deep sleep. Mother dropped off, too; the night before none of the grown-ups had undressed.

That night we children went to bed very early. Tired out by the previous night's wakefulness I was sound asleep almost before my head touched the pillow.

We were in fact all fast asleep in the nursery while Father lived through his last minutes. He awoke about ten in the evening; Mother was there beside his bed anxiously watching his face.

Father smiled faintly and in a quiet but firm voice told Mother that he had something important to say to her before he died. Mother burst into tears and, smothering his hands with kisses, begged him not to think about death—especially now when he was stronger after his sleep and must be getting better; but Father shook his head and said that he had little strength left. He begged Mother not to 'torture him with priests' but to call Nanny in because he had a few words to say to her.

Mother was so used to believing Father in everything, that she did so now. Unable to control her despair, she threw herself on her knees beside his bed, crying and shouting until Nanny picked her up and calmed her. Father was so upset by her outburst that for a long time he could not speak, but when her sobs died down he gathered his strength. First of all he thanked her for the happiness she had brought him during the past twenty years; then slowly, and in detail, he went over his affairs with her. The situation was serious; he was deeply in debt, but had been hoping to make repayment gradually out of his salary. Now, he said, Mother would have to sell the best part of the estate after his death to pay off his debts. There was not enough money for to her to engage an experienced bailiff, and from now on she would have to manage on her own but for the help of the foreman from the village —but he assured her that as soon as she started managing the estate her intelligence and natural ability would tell her what to do and she would run it far better than he, who had brought her to her present condition.

Here Father sighed deeply and, turning to Nanny, said he hoped she would be the guardian angel not only of his children, but also of his wife, and would become her right hand in all she did.

'My last request', he said to Mother in an almost inaudible voice, 'is: educate the children. Do it even if you have to sell the whole of the estate. Before I die I have just one more thing to ask: be kind to the peasants. Let no one do them any harm and never give them cause to curse you in their misery.' His strength was gone and he could speak no more.

For a moment Mother and Nanny stood by the bed unable to move; and when Mother did bend over him he was no longer breathing.

I was woken up that night by Sasha shouting: 'Get up—something's happened!' We jumped out of bed and stood listening; doors were being slammed all over the house, feet were running up and down the corridors, things were being carried in and out, servants' names were being shouted. From the far end of the house came screams and sobs, and then we heard the sound of many footsteps together, as though something cumbersome were being carried out. . . . When the noise subsided a little, Sasha said she would go and see what it was all about.

'I'll come with you.'

'Me too!'

'I'm not staying here by myself.'

We were all round Sasha, shouting. Hanging on to her we ran barefoot and in our nightshirts out into the corridor. Opposite us was a door leading into the hall with a narrow streak of light beneath it. Sasha flung the door open, we went in and stood petrified: Father lay dead on a table in the middle of the room, dressed in his clothes and with lit wax candles all around him.

One of us screamed and the others joined in. At that moment Nanny ran into the hall from the opposite door: when she saw us she stretched out her arms and, trying to enfold all of us, began to sob. 'Poor darlings,' she murmured. 'Orphans . . . you poor, poor mites.' Then, suddenly realizing we had no shoes on and only our nightshirts, dragged us all back into the nursery.

Father's funeral was hardly over when two of my sisters went down with cholera; they were buried one after the other. In the next three weeks the epidemic took four more children from the family. Our elders were so busy looking after the sick and making arrangements for funerals that those of us who escaped infection were completely neglected.

Nobody stopped us from running into the rooms of those who were ill, so it is not surprising that the illness spread fast.

For four or five weeks nobody in the house had a proper night's rest and Mother and Nanny could hardly move for exhaustion and despair, but three or four days after the last funeral Mother began to hurry our move to the country. A man was sent to Pogoreloye on horseback to warn the peasants we were coming, and some of them had to bring carts into the town to transport all our belongings: but before packing started in earnest a good rest was decided on. 'Go and get some sleep', Mother told Nanny: 'you can hardly stand.'

However, before going to her room, Nanny went to the servants' quarters and told the maids to light the nursery stoves and keep an eye on the children. There weren't many of us left by now—only fifteen-year-old Nyuta, twelve-year-old Sasha, two brothers (Andrei and Zarya), myself and a seven-year-old sister, Nina. Nyuta, who had been helping the grown-ups, also lay down to sleep while Sasha, Andrei and Zarya went into the garden.

When the maid saw that not only Mother and Nanny but even Nyuta was asleep she calmly disobeyed her orders and went back to the servants' quarters. Nina and I decided to do our dolls' washing and we found a basin, poured water into it, and started work. Presently Nina announced that she had finished her washing and, holding the wet rags in her hands, began to dry them in front of the roaring fire in the open stove.

Suddenly there was a dreadful scream and as I turned I was horrified to see that her flimsy frock was on fire. Still screaming, she ran into the other room; I ran after her but suddenly everything went dark. It felt as though the floor had disappeared under my feet, and I fell down unconscious.

When I came to, I was lying on my bed and Nina, swathed

in bandages, was on the other bed against the opposite wall. The doctor arrived immediately but nothing could be done for her; she had been very badly burned and died a few days later.

After Nina's funeral—the eighth in the family—I remained in bed dangerously ill. Terrible stomach pains and vomiting showed I had cholera. I cannot remember how long I was ill or whether I suffered much; my memories of the time are very disjointed, but I do know that after pains and convulsions I fell at one point into a coma and could neither speak nor move. Nanny did not leave my bedside, and when she rubbed my chilly feet or straightened my pillows I could feel her hot tears falling on to my face. Seeing me lie there motionless made her frightened and she began to call to me, begging me to say a word or even just nod my head if I could hear her; but I made no movement—either from obstinacy or a genuine lack of strength, I can't remember which. Eventually Nanny called loudly to Mother, who came in quickly, sat on the edge of my bed, and put her hand on my forehead.

'She's dying,' said Mother in a voice that was barely audible.

'God forbid!' cried Nanny: 'We must rub her . . . I shan't let her. We must rub her. Call the doctor—Madam dear, do call the doctor!'

But Mother did not move. She sat as if in a trance, shaking her head and saying over and over again: 'It's the ninth death, the ninth death! Well, what of it—let her die. There's nothing left to feed them with.'

Too young to understand her words properly, I did not sense the bitterness and despair in them. Afraid by moving to show that I could hear everything, I lay with my face buried in the pillow as a heavy lump came in my throat and the tears choked me. 'My mother, my own mother wants me to die,' I repeated to myself: 'My mother, my own mother does not love me!'

Even before this incident I had been more attached to
Nanny than to my mother, but these words uttered so un-
guardedly at a moment of despair often afterwards produced
a fury and resentment in me towards her and darkened my
childhood with many black hours.

And so our family misfortunes came to an end. The house
was sold to a merchant and the money used to pay off our
debts: now we could go. Packing took up a few days more,
with everybody busy from morning to night—we were
taking with us all we possessed, for we were leaving the town
for good.

The estate at Pogoreloye was fifty miles away. In order to
move all our belongings including the town furniture—as
well as us, the maids, the valets, the cooks, the coachmen and
the washerwomen—a series of horse-drawn carts was sent
from the country. To transport the 'master's family' there
was sent a *dormez*, a cumbersome great wagon on high wheels,
covered over with cracked and faded leather fixed to the
wood by ordinary rusty nails; holes cut in the side for windows had curtains drawn across in bad weather but were left
open when it was fine. Inside, the wagon was lined with a
grey material padded and quilted by serf-girls with cotton-
wool.

What dozens of bags and pockets and compartments there
were inside the wagon! There were pockets for towels, for
bottles of *kvas* and milk, for mugs, matches, soap, combs
and brushes. In spite of the fact that its capacious lining was
stuffed with the various necessities for travel, boxes of provisions stood in all the corners and bags and bundles stuffed
with the results of sundry bakings and roastings dangled from
the roof. When the road was rough and the coach swayed
badly, bottles and bundles fell out of their places and on to
the heads of the travellers.

Living Above Our Means

The bottom of the wagon was filled with straw and feather-beds and cushions were placed on top. Lying down was more comfortable than sitting—even a grown man could stretch out on it. Of course one could not make the whole journey lying down, but sitting up entailed rearranging everything all over again—moving every box, bundle and parcel and folding up all the blankets and pillows. We children christened our wagon the Noah's Ark.

It was only a two-day journey, but enough provisions were prepared to feed an entire regiment on the march. From early morning on the day before we left, things began to be assembled in the hall; first boxes of biscuits packed in cardboard filled the room with the smell of singed paper, then a dish covered with buns of various kinds, now roast geese, chicken and young pullets. And the pies that were prepared for the occasion! Pies with carrots and potatoes, pies with meat fillings, even the sort of pie which has a tiny chicken rolled up whole inside.

The day of our departure had arrived. In the street in front of our house the loaded carts stood ready. The wagon was brought to the porch. For the last time we gathered in the dining-room in order to sit down before the journey in the old Russian tradition.

When Mother came in she sat behind us but suddenly fell to her knees with a groan. 'Why did it have to happen, why?' she cried, sobbing desperately. Then she rose quickly and went first into her husband's study, then into the room which had been her dead children's, crying hopelessly as she went. Gathered in Nanny's arms we children began sobbing too; but gradually Mother's terrible crying subsided and she came out, her face blotchy and her eyes swollen with tears. Breathing heavily she leant against the wall as though in need of support; then, making an effort, she straightened up and gave the order to start.

Our move into the country looked like the flight out of Egypt. Twenty carts loaded with our belongings and with cattle tethered to the tailboards crowded along one behind the other. The horses pulling our wagon had bells on their harness—the bell on the middle one was beautifully big and clear—but the three of them harnessed side by side and driven by the coachman could not manage the heavy vehicle by themselves: two more were harnessed in front and driven by a peasant astride one of them. When the horses started a tremendous noise broke out—shoutings and crashings and janglings of big bells and small. We thoroughly enjoyed it, of course, but I doubt if the same could be said of Mother, who was feeling rather weak.

Mother lay down on one side of the wagon, I was put next to her and Nanny snuggled down beside me; my two brothers and two sisters sat facing us. Nina's death meant that only five of us were left.

At first the road was good and we moved fairly quickly. Nanny had given us all some nuts in an attempt to prevent our feeling bored; we cracked them with our teeth and threw the shells out of the window, for as the weather was good the curtains were pulled back. However, potholes and bumps became more frequent and we kept on being jolted about. Andrei stood upright, saying that when the coach jerked the nuts cracked themselves in one's mouth, and at that moment a sharp jolt nearly threw him over. He clutched at a string holding a bottle of *kvas*: it came away, the bottle broke and the liquid spilled over our feet.

Mother pulled herself up angrily and told the coachman to stop. Then she smacked my brother angrily across the face and shouted: 'You fool, don't you know how to behave in front of your mother? Get into the servants' wagon.'

Now Andrei was the eldest son. Already a pupil at the Military Academy, he only came home for the summer vacation. Considering himself very much our senior he liked to order the servants about and spoke to them in a way which in our house even the grown-ups never used. All this made travelling with the servants a humiliating punishment for him, but we put him down and continued our journey.

The distance between our estate and the village where we spent the night was only about twenty miles, but it was the most difficult part of the journey and we had to get across Devil's Bridge. Actually there wasn't even a road, much less a bridge, so how it got its name is far from clear; the ground was marshy and only roughly filled in with dry brushwood, rubble and stones. Tree stumps and enormous boulders stuck out here and there, and large pot-holes full of greenish mud glistened in the sun.

As we neared Devil's Bridge the coachman stopped the horses and came up to the little window by which Mother was lying, and told her that the first horse and cart he had sent ahead to test the road had already got stuck; they would have to be extricated and the road mended. All the servants jumped down and started to work—some chopped down brushwood and saplings at the side of the road and piled them into the pot-holes and puddles while others inserted long logs under the wheels of the bogged-down cart to get it out of the mud. At last horse and cart were free and the road made a little better; we could go on, and it was decided to send off the carts first one at a time. As soon as one began to sink men ran up and pulled it left or right by tugging the horse's bridle—often sinking into the mud to their knees or even their waists in the process.

Our wagon stood by the road waiting its turn; the last cart was across and now we could start. Once more it started its squeaks, creaks and desperate groans. Two men threw brushwood into the pot-holes and puddles in front, and to help the tiring horses our servants pushed at the sides and the back.

More than once we had to stop to free the horses from the mud but somehow the crossing of Devil's Bridge was achieved.

At last the hellish road was ended. Men and horses were completely exhausted and to give them a rest Mother ordered a stop at the next village, although Pogoreloye was only ten miles or so farther on.

We drove into our estate that evening; having been too young the year before to retain anything in my memory I had completely forgotten the village, but as soon as our enormous magnificent lake at the foot of the mountain and our big country house came into view Nanny lifted me up to the window. 'Look, look,' she said. 'There's our lake, and the house too; look at it shining in the sun, just like a real palace!'

Women and children were standing with gifts on the steps of the house; the women handed Mother bread and salt and eggs and the children had bunches of wild-flowers for my sisters and me, and they also gave us a live baby hare and a pair of young birds.

Mother walked about the rooms as if she were seeing them for the first time; the tears poured down her face as she gave a few absent-minded orders. Presently she went into a small room with a single window built on to the side of the house, and after a few minutes called Nanny and me in; as we entered she snatched me into her arms and smothered me with kisses. Her hot tears fell on my face and arms.

'Liza, darling,' she said at last, 'I'm going to give this room to you and Nanny. You're the youngest in the family now and not so strong as the others, so you need her the most.'

I was overjoyed to think that now Nanny would be with me for always, for I understood Mother to mean that she was giving Nanny to me and that from then on she would belong to me alone.

2

Making the Estate Pay

So began a new phase in my life. For us children, the move into the country was naturally wonderful; the spacious house was airy and comfortable with side-rooms leading off the corridors, there were separate out-buildings in the yard, a large shady garden with winding paths and beyond it a broad field and the blue lake at the foot of the mountain. It was all so attractive, with so many possibilities in the way of games and walks, that it could scarcely be compared to what we had in Porechye.

Mother gave herself up completely to managing the estate and had no time for us children. In the families of the big landowners little attention was ever paid to children, and there was no real contact between them and their parents. In the morning the children kissed their parents' hands and wished them 'Good morning'; after dinner and supper they kissed their hands again and thanked them for their meal; before going to bed they wished them 'Good night', and that was the limit of the day's exchanges between parent and child.

Governesses and nurses kept a strict watch to see that children did not annoy their elders, and for the slightest offence they had their heads smacked or were thrashed with a cane. It was not surprising that the children were always longing to be in the servants' quarters, where life was much more fun as maids, valets and coachmen ate, gossiped, discussed and debated the other country families—and where there were always bits of turnip and cabbage lying about that one could nibble on the quiet.

There was a superstition in those days that black cockroaches were lucky and brought about early marriages, with the result that mothers with marriageable daughters tried to encourage the cockroaches to breed by putting breadcrumbs and sugar behind the skirting boards. Where this was done the cockroaches fell on to the children as they slept at night; and of course there were always bugs and fleas in abundance.

Life was far from pleasant. After we lost our fortune Mother began to introduce strict economies everywhere, and in the evenings we sat in the half-light without candles until it was pitch-dark outside; and although the candles we did have were made from our own animal fat and not bought, even they were strictly rationed. In the whole of the house only two candles were lit each evening, one on the dining-room table round which we children sat with Mother and Nanny and the other in the servants' hall.

This, however, was not the worst deprivation we children suffered. . . . We used to discuss with real regret the sweets that nobody gave us nowadays, though of course such conversations could only be held with Mother out of the room.

'Why do we never have whipped cream or biscuits nowadays?' we used to ask Nanny. 'We have our own cream and eggs, there's no need to buy any.'

'Because we have to go carefully with sugar and flour,' she would say. 'In any case there's no time to fuss about with that kind of thing now. And don't worry your Mother about it, for the Lord's sake don't irritate her.'

Occasionally, however, we had a windfall; and this is what used to happen. In our household, preserves used to be made for the winter from honey and treacle, and various cordials prepared from the local berries; but a proportion of what we made, particularly if treacle had been used in it, always went bad. Nanny used to show each pot of spoiled jam or curd to Mother who would taste it, sigh heavily, and say something such as: 'What a pity! It really is completely spoiled. . . . Well, give it to the children.' And, in order to prolong our enjoyment rather than from the fear that too much might make us sick, she would order each of us to be given just a little saucer of it: so for weeks and months we would eat every day jam so sour that the whole room reeked of it.

The same thing happened with every other kind of food in the house: if it was actually covered with mildew it went out to the servants, but what was only slightly affected was given to the children.

We always awaited with impatience the time when the honeycombs were cut from the bee-hives, an operation which took place in the height of summer. We used to run out on to the porch from where we could watch old Miron the gardener walking to the hives. He wore special clothes on these occasions—a thing over his head like a mask, made of thick leather with holes for eyes and mouth, and long heavy gloves on his hands. He carried a clean wooden tray on which were a spoon, a knife and a flat blade. The bees swarmed all over him but mask and gloves protected him so well that he was never stung.

When the honeycombs had been extracted they were brought into the dining-room, where Mother and Nanny put them into special crocks. At the side of each crock near the bottom there was a hole stopped with a wooden bung. Crocks full of honeycombs were placed on high stools; at the side of each was another lower stool on which stood an ordinary pot without a hole. The bung was then removed from the upper crock so that clear honey dripped down into the pot below.

Holidays, that is to say days when Mother was at home, were always chosen for this operation. If she had to go out the dining-room door was always locked immediately, but this did not deter us. Having seen her clear of the house our Cadet (that is what we called Andrei) opened the dining-room window from the garden and climbed easily through into the locked room while the rest of us held our breath and watched his every movement. When he was sure that the coast was clear, Andrei signalled to us and we hurried into the dining-room in turn. As the smallest, I was lifted up by the others. We rushed to the crocks and thrust our palms under the dripping honey, licked our hands and put them again and again under the sweet trickle.

Neither seeing us in the garden nor hearing our voices indoors, Nanny used to guess what we were up to. Terrified that Mother would find out, she would run up to the window and call in a frightened whisper: 'Your mother's coming . . . just you wait, I'll tell her everything.' Then we would get frightened and jump out; none of us was scared of Nanny, of course, but we were afraid of Mother. We calmed down as soon as we realized there was no sign of her, but Nanny would go on shaking with fright for us. 'You are a wicked boy, Andrei,' she would tell my brother. 'I'll cross myself out of sheer thankfulness when you go back to college. Nice things you're teaching your brothers and sisters! I don't know what would happen if the servants saw you and told your mother.'

Mother used to rise at dawn and leave the house for the fields at once. We never saw her until dinner-time when she returned home worn out, and we would go up to her one after the other to kiss her hand.

Making the Estate Pay

She always greeted us with the same hasty question: 'Well, are you all right? Been for a walk?' Often she would ask the question on a cold wet day when we could not have left the house, but the fact had not registered; nor did she notice that sometimes we did not answer her, or gave her only a sulky glance. She was completely preoccupied with her new work: estate management took precedence over all her other anxieties and she had no time left to think of anything else.

When it was time for dinner or supper, Nanny would run out on to the porch and shout to us to come in. Meal-times were rigidly fixed, and if any of us was late and only arrived in time for the second or third course, his was served with everybody else's and he was not given those he had missed . . . but actually we were never very worried about missing a course. As soon as everyone left the table, Nanny quietly drew the culprit aside into one of the side-rooms or the pantry where often one might find oneself eating cold borsch after fruit and milk, with possibly a couple of eggs and a slice of ham to follow! Nanny was always afraid that we might go hungry.

Usually it was my brothers who were late. Andrei might either be visiting one of the neighbours or going shooting with them: no one knew where he went or whom he was friendly with. Nine-year-old Zarya often followed him.

But if my brothers were rarely at home, we girls hardly ever left it. I used to follow Nanny everywhere. If she went to the barn to give out some flour or grain or cereal, I covered myself with a shawl and followed her; if she sat in a side-room knitting, I squatted at her feet. My elder sister Nyuta was constantly embroidering trimmings and collars, transferring patterns or making designs for embroidery, or going into the kitchen to cook something or busying herself in the garden planting flowers or hoeing round the shrubs. As for my sister Sasha, she sat with bowed head studying her books.

A Russian Childhood

Father had always insisted to Mother that Sasha was a very gifted child, and from her earliest years she showed an extraordinary capacity for learning, making brilliant progress in both general studies and music. When we lived at Porechye Father had given her lessons and she had also had visiting teachers. She read and wrote well and spoke both French and German fairly fluently; under Father's guidance she had read many classics in these languages and Russian, and had worked hard on written compositions in all three.

Having lost Father, Sasha was left without a guide—but was determined to continue her education at all costs. Not knowing how to set about it she began to read all the books Father had left; but his library had suffered a good deal during our move and in any case most of the volumes were too difficult for her. Sasha did not despair but threw herself into her brother's textbooks—where she foundered faster than ever. As Andrei was often away from the house all day, Sasha used to sit from the morning onwards in the room with windows facing the yard. From this observation point she could not miss him, and as soon as he appeared she would leave her post, snatch up a notebook she had prepared or a book open at a particular page, and rush to him.

'Just a moment, Andrei,' she would call: 'just one little moment'—and beg her brother to explain some problem she could not understand; but Andrei rarely bothered to do what she asked.

'Miserable wretch!' he would exclaim with theatrical horror. 'You'll get the reputation of a bluestocking!'

But Sasha, refusing to be put off, would clutch at his sleeve and rattle off her questions. Usually Andrei tore himself away with a shout of 'Oh, go to hell—I don't know anything about it myself,' and vanished through the garden gate.

Sasha, once so gay and animated, was becoming neurotic, morose and irritable. She would run suddenly from her books to the piano, spend some time working on a piece of music, and then rush and throw herself weeping on her bed. Mother was never at home so that if anyone came to console her it was Nanny, whose heart was near to breaking over Sasha's despair.

Nanny puzzled for a long time over the best way to help. She questioned the neighbours about the possibilities of arranging Sasha's education and eventually went over to see Mme Voinov, who—together with Mother—was considered one of the best educated women in the district.

The subsequent conversations she had with her made Nanny realize the full difficulty of being some help to Sasha. Mother could not afford boarding-school fees and it was almost impossible to get into a government-run institution. Nanny was very depressed with this information but she suddenly had an idea: she would write a letter to the Tsar.

For a long time she told nobody of her plan, but she couldn't put it into operation without help. Apart from not knowing how such things were done she couldn't even write, so she decided to tell the parish priest everything and ask him to write the petition for her. She imagined that all that had to be done to persuade the Tsar to fulfil her request was to provide him with a straightforward account of Mother's difficulties—how she had been left a widow and was ruining her health in the attempt to provide her children with a living. 'You must put in that the deceased gentleman found Sasha very talented,' Nanny told the priest, 'and everybody knows what a brain *he* had.'

That was Nanny's idea; but the priest—having accepted a present of two young chickens from her—decided otherwise. Such a petition, he said immediately, would get nowhere; Father's position had not been important enough. He refused to write a petition to the Tsar but suggested that Mother should get in touch with her brothers and ask them to do something for Sasha and get her accepted into a school. As he bade her good-bye he suggested that Nanny should bring Sasha along to him so that he could give her some assistance in her studies.

Nanny and Sasha and I went to the priest's house the next day—Sasha carrying a well-thumbed arithmetic book and several textbooks under her arm. The priest met us hospitably and offered us refreshments, and his wife brought in a whole crowd of children so that I should not be bored. However, I refused to leave Nanny's skirts and she had to come outside with me: left behind with the priest, Sasha opened her books at once and together they bent over them.

She came out an hour later, lips pressed tightly together and a frown on her forehead. Seeing her expression Nanny hurriedly began her farewells and we walked home in a long silence; Nanny was afraid that if she asked questions Sasha might be still more upset.

On the way back we sat down for a rest. Sasha laid her head on Nanny's lap and burst into bitter weeping—but at that moment we heard the noise of wheels and saw the 'karafashka', which was our private name for the little trap Mother used for driving round the estate. Mother was returning home from the fields: when she saw us she told the driver to stop and we got in beside her.

Although Mother paid little attention to us she did notice Sasha's red eyes at once. Nanny began to explain that we had been visiting the priest so that Sasha could get some help from him in her studies but Sasha interrupted and, fighting back her tears with difficulty, began to upbraid Mother for never giving a thought to her education—with the result that she had had to go to the priest, who would only explain a few mathematical problems to her. When she had asked him to explain something else he told her that there was no need for a girl to know so much—she already knew more than was good for her and educated women were only a laughing-stock. Andrei, Sasha added, only laughed at her and called her a bluestocking.

'Andrei's a good-for-nothing and the priest is a fool,' Mother broke in. 'The more you know the more money you can earn. It's a governess's life for you.' But she was not cross with my sister for her reproaches.

We rode the rest of the way in silence. Mother was deep in thought and Nanny judged that her moment was here; as soon as we got out of the 'karafashka' Nanny began to talk to her, and passed on the priest's suggestion that she should approach her brothers for help.

That same day Nanny, shaking with joy and excitement, sent off a letter to St. Petersburg. Sasha, it was decided, should be told nothing.

Meanwhile, Mother was completely absorbed in problems of management, and her efforts to run the estate as efficiently as possible involved the continual introduction of new rules. She had a lot of trouble with many of the serfs, and the most difficult of all turned out to be Vaska the musician.

Twelve or thirteen years previously my father had started to notice a young village lad. Wherever people gathered together at holiday time Vaska—that was his name—would be there, and even peasants in neighbouring villages invited him to play at their weddings. Being fond of music my father took an interest in his playing and one day made Vaska bring all his musical instruments to his study and play to him. When he had demonstrated his home-made violin, balalaika, concertina and various flutes and whistles, Father asked him to play something on a really good violin he had borrowed from somewhere for the occasion.

The result was amazing. Vaska spent a long time tuning it and trying something out and then suddenly began to play a

Chopin nocturne. Asked by my astonished father where he had learned it, he explained that a lady who often played it on the piano had been a guest in the house last summer; he used to stand under the window listening, and had never forgotten the 'tune', but could not manage to play it on his home-made violin.

From that moment Vaska's fate was settled. Father wrote about him to Prince G., an old friend of his who was one of the richest landowners in our part of the country. Father knew that the prince had recently returned from abroad and, having settled down on their country estate with his wife, a keen musician, had decided to organize a private orchestra— going so far as to hire foreign teachers to train his serfs. The prince gladly accepted Vaska into his orchestra and two years later began to beg my father to sell him. The boy, he wrote, had turned out to be an exceptionally gifted person—he had learned to read and write very quickly, enjoyed books, and had a genuine talent for music. But my father, who was thinking of forming his own theatre, refused point-blank and shortly afterwards took Vaska back.

While my father was alive Vaska could live the life of an artist and no other claims were made on his time. Tall, thin and slightly round-shouldered, and with big thoughtful eyes, Vaska was like a peasant in neither appearance nor speech. It was hardly surprising; he was literate, had read a little and learned a lot—partly in the prince's service and partly in my father's theatre. He married our maid Minodora, who was a perfect match for him. A member of our household since she was very small, Minodora was the same age as my elder sisters who had died of cholera and had spent a lot of her time with them; she had taken parts in several of our plays, could read and write, and had a pleasant even temperament which endeared her to every member of the household.

However, times had changed now for both Vaska and

Minodora. His music was no longer wanted in the house; it only irritated Mother, and the poor lad had to try to keep out of her way. For days on end he did not dare risk provoking her anger by touching his violin. Only during the warm summer evenings when the lights were out around the farm, in the servants' cottages and in the Big House would Vaska steal into the hay-loft and play his violin, blowing softly on a little whistle held between his lips as he played.

Sasha was the only person on the whole estate who appreciated Vaska's playing. She saw a reflection of her own unhappy lot in his miserable fate, and this added to the sympathy and pity she felt for him. Often when she heard the sound of his violin Sasha would beg Nanny to take us up to him in the hay-loft, and we would clamber up on to the hay and listen to his music for hours.

Meanwhile Mother went on introducing her reforms, and as soon as all the house servants were settled into their new jobs she started on Vaska with all the severity and obstinacy her dominating personality could muster. Vaska must choose: he was either to be hired out to some trade or to take a plot of land and settle down to cultivate it.

He was at his wits' end, continually dashing between the servants' quarters and the house, whispering with his Minodora, coming to Mother begging her to give him a piece of land and then refusing both to take it and to be hired out. He desperately wanted to join a theatre orchestra in a town, but he was afraid he had not had enough training for it; and in any case he had forgotten a good deal since he first studied music. Another thing was that he was afraid nobody knew him well enough to give him a job.

Mother's displeasure with Vaska was extended to his wife. Previously Minodora had had only sewing and tidying up the rooms to do, but now she had to take on all the heavy work single-handed. Being unused to it, and not particularly strong in any case, she found it difficult to cope with the new work. This infuriated Mother still more, and Minodora's position grew daily more precarious. The fear of having to work as a peasant if Vaska were forced to take the land, anxiety over him, together with endless coughs and colds completely ruined her health—despite which she always tried to appear healthy and vigorous. When she had to run out into the yard on some errand she never dared cover herself with a shawl even in rain or snow in case it brought reproaches on her head for acting the lady.

One day after supper Mother was told that Vaska was asking to see her. Guessing why, she ordered Louka the bailiff to be called in. Mother never made any decisions over managing the estate without consulting him; he served her faithfully and honestly, and the respect and honour she showed him made him work harder than ever.

'Well,' Mother asked Vaska sternly, 'what have you to say?'

He explained that he had definitely decided not to take the piece of land.

'But only the other day you begged me to let you have a piece near the meadow,' said Mother. 'I can't countermand my orders every day just because you have a mind like a grasshopper. I've already given Louka an order to supply you with wood for building—and you can take your wife with you, I don't need her. You can settle down on the land like all the rest have done—and if you don't want to, you'll be hired out. Now, for the last time—choose which you want!'

Vaska threw himself at her feet in tears and begged her to listen to him.

'As God's my witness, Madam, I can neither work the land nor bring you money from being hired out. I never shirked the work when I was a young lad, Madam—I used to plough and make hay and everything else. Then the master, God rest him, made me go in for music, and I did: but now it's thirteen years since I left the land, and how can I go back to it after all that? Then the music, Madam: I spent two and a half years studying it, but then I was taken into the prince's orchestra straight from the plough and long were the weeks I lost getting myself accustomed to the new life. It's true I learned to read music, Madam, but if I applied to join a town orchestra I'd be expected to be note-perfect. . . . How can I do it, Madam? The master never let me carry on with my studies—he put me on to teaching others what I had learned to play myself—no, he wouldn't let me go on with my training, and now at night I have to dry my tears with my fists because of it. I didn't whine, though; I didn't argue about it—but how can I earn money for you with my violin? Have pity on us, Madam, let my wife and me stay with you; I swear to God we will serve you faithfully.'

'Have you gone crazy?' Mother shouted: 'What do you think you can do, play me your songs as I come home from the fields? If on your admission you didn't learn music well enough to earn your living when you were at the prince's, you're downright lazy and a fool into the bargain. For two and a half years you contributed nothing to this household, two and a half years were wasted on this idiotic training— and now, if you please, nothing has come of it. You could have gone on strumming away at your songs without all that training and been some use to us at the same time. Let me tell you this: I shan't hire you out, I know you'll bring me no profit that way, but don't think I'm going to keep you and your wife for nothing. You're going to learn to plough and thresh and work on the land with me. And now you may go.'

When the door shut behind Vaska, Mother turned to the bailiff: 'Well, what have you to say now?' she asked.

'What *can* I say, Ma'am? Don't take on, now, but I'll lay no good'll ever come of any job *he* ever does. Of course, it's for you to say, Ma'am, but the fact is I've lost all patience with the fellow. Yesterday you sent word to have the grass cut in the field on t'other side of the kitchen garden. Well, I sent Petrok along too and you wouldn't credit the time poor Petrok had with him. He's a witless lad, and that's the truth, but I'm sure I don't know what's best done with him. Of course, Ma'am, this may be your way of taking it out on me because I didn't take proper account of this and that—making me play wet-nurse to this Vaska. But I do beg you to take him off my hands, Ma'am, for I can't abide the fellow and that's God's truth.'

'Oh, no!' cried Mother. 'Do take pity on me! Does this mean I shall have to keep him and his wife for nothing?'

'There's no call to do that, Ma'am. You can put him at something or other—building repairs, or maybe wood-cutting. And if he turns out useless at everything, there's still one thing as you can do.'

'And what might that be?'

'Follow your neighbours' example, Ma'am. There's nothing like a good thrashing to knock the daftness out of a man.'

Mother had practically reached the conclusion that it was the only thing to be done with Vaska, but she hesitated to give the order. Her husband's last requests were clear in her mind and she respected them, but to make sure that Vaska earned his bread she began to watch his every step. When he went threshing, she went too: 'You fool!' she would shout as, instead of the straw, he hit his neighbour's feet with the flail; and when, put in the front rank of reapers with the best men, he blunted two of the finest scythes in succession, she was so angry that she stamped her feet at him with rage. He was no more useful when it came to building work; once he was put to plane planks and almost immediately the bailiff came to report that Vaska had ruined the plane. After each mishap Vaska was called indoors, where Mother scolded him unmercifully.

Making the Estate Pay

On one such occasion Mother warned him that if he did no better she would send him into the Army. Vaska was hurt and terrified.

'What is that for, Madam?' he asked. 'Perhaps you will still manage to get rid of me some other way: there might be someone who would give you good money for me.'

'How dare you talk such rubbish! Who on earth would be silly enough to want your idiotic music?'

The most suitable job for Vaska—sensible, honest and literate—was really carrying out the household's most complicated errands. Almost every day the bailiff would ask Mother's permission to send him to the blacksmith to arrange for the repair of some broken tool or to have a horse shod, or perhaps to the mill. He was also despatched on various household tasks—to the district council with letters, or to buy things, or even perhaps into town. Vaska executed these commissions so well that Mother began considering a way of making even better use of his abilities.

In spite of the fact that we existed almost entirely on the produce of the estate, there was a certain amount of surplus—butter, oats, rye and various kinds of livestock: calves, for instance, and pigs. Several times Mother had tried to sell these items in nearby towns or to various innkeepers, but so little was made on the transactions that she did not consider them really worth while. Now she decided to try once more and sent Vaska with the produce. Imagine her amazement when he returned and laid on the table a sum four times bigger than what she had been receiving previously—and produced at the same time a careful note of what he had sold and where and for what price. Mother was astounded. She immediately called in the peasants who had handled the sales before and berated them as thieves and cheats for pocketing her money.

After that Vaska began to travel into town regularly and his sales always resulted in a profit. Although Mother had not yet made a final decision as to the fate of Vaska and Mino-dora, we children (who were very fond of them both) at last felt less anxious about them. Sasha was more pleased than the rest of us: Vaska's gift for music, even more than his kindness to her, touched her to the heart.

When autumn came it was time to send Andrei back to college. Vaska was to take him there and deliver him into the hands of the authorities, and in the evenings Nanny would mention to Mother every now and again how nice it was to have a reliable man like Vaska.

Mother was sad and silent; parting from Andrei grieved her. In spite of the fact that he was the most disobedient of all her children and was often even impertinent to her, and that she disliked his tendency to put on airs, Andrei was her favourite child.

Andrei's going meant almost nothing to us children; we saw so little of him when he was at home. Only Sasha cried; but she was not upset by her brother's departure, her tears were for her own fate. 'Everybody's studying except me,' she said again and again through her sobs. 'I shall have to spend the rest of my life in this hole.'

Vaska returned a week later, having picked up a money order for us on his way back. Mother turned over the mysterious slip of paper in her hands for a long time: somebody had sent her three hundred roubles.

Nanny was the first to guess. 'Madam, dear, it must be from your brothers. You wrote to them about Sasha's studies, and this is the money they are sending for them. Only please let's not say a word about it to Sasha, she's become so weak and thin and irritable that the excitement will be too much for her. When we're quite sure we'll get her used to the idea gradually.'

That evening Nanny began gently to prepare my sister: 'Sasha, my dear, kneel down before the icons and pray that a dream I had comes true. I dreamed that you were going away to a school to study.'

'But I don't *want* to pray. I don't and I won't. D'you hear me, I shall never pray again, never!' shouted Sasha crossly, and then fell suddenly to the floor where she thrashed about crying and shouting.

Next morning Mother received the letter. She hurried nervously to open it—and knew from the opening words that Nanny had guessed correctly. Mother's brothers, our uncles in St. Petersburg, advised her to send Sasha to the *pensionnat* of Mme Kotto in Vitebsk, then considered a model of its kind for young ladies, and were sending the money for this purpose.

Nanny and Mother whispered together for a long time over how to tell my sister; after the previous day's fit Sasha looked pale and exhausted. In the end Mother called her in and told her that her brothers had written promising to help get her into a *pensionnat*.

'But I know nothing will ever come of it,' Sasha interrupted at once; and, rushing out of Mother's room, threw herself on her bed. When Mother came in a minute later she was fast asleep. She did not wake her, and Mother let her sleep all day; in the evening Sasha allowed herself to be undressed and put into bed without opening her eyes.

When Sasha came into our room the next morning, Nanny deliberately said to me in a loud voice: 'Our Sasha will go away to study, you'll see . . . she'll learn all sorts of things and she'll teach you as well. There, she doesn't believe me, but Mother left her a letter to read before she went out. We didn't tell her everything, but we've got the money already!'

She looked at Sasha. 'Well, dear, why don't you say something? Take the letter!'

Lips pressed tightly together, Sasha took the letter in silence and left the room unhurriedly.

Nanny was frightened. 'Merciful heavens!' she exclaimed. 'What can be the matter with her? Such wonderful news, and she took no pleasure in it. There'll be trouble, God save us.'

At this moment Nyuta ran in. 'Nanny,' she cried, 'there's something wrong with Sasha. I was so happy she'd got her wish and I wanted to talk to her about it, but she won't say anything, she looks as if she's in a trance.'

We rushed in to Sasha; she was sitting with bent head, looking pale and sleepy.

'What's the matter with you, Sasha dear?' Nanny asked. 'Do tell me, darling; just say one word. Have you a headache or something?'

'I'm so sleepy,' Sasha answered in a barely audible whisper. 'Do leave me alone.'

This alarmed Nanny. 'How can you be sleepy?' she demanded. 'You slept all day yesterday, and all through the night; you've only just got up, and now you want to go to sleep again. . . . Nyuta, go and get some smelling salts and give them to her while I rub her feet for her.'

But Sasha only begged to be left in peace, and Nanny ran to the servants' quarters and told Vaska to hurry out to the fields and fetch Mother home.

'Well, what is it now?' Mother almost shouted when Nanny ran out to her as she came home. 'Your God must have got bored because we've managed to get through a few months without a disaster.' In moments of stress Mother always reproached Nanny about 'her' God.

'Madam, dear, how can you say such things! We must submit ourselves humbly . . .'

'To hell with you and your humility,' Mother shouted furiously as she tore off her coat. 'I've been humble long enough. I've been so humble it made me blind. I didn't see that my own daughter was wasting away from grief.'

And she rushed into Sasha's room, where she threw herself

on to her knees at the bedside, kissing Sasha's hands and sobbing: 'Forgive me, forgive me . . . my daughter, my darling.'

Sasha lifted herself up, but her head fell back on to the
pillow. 'Do leave me alone,' she said with some difficulty.
'I'm so sleepy.'

'Oh, God!' cried Mother. 'Why should I have to go on
living if they are all to die? No, this I cannot bear.'

Mother's despair and her fear for Sasha's life took me back
to my illness and I remembered the time she had said so
thoughtlessly: 'Let her die!' Overcome with anger and bitterness I ran over to her, bent down, and bit her hand as hard as
I could—and rushed out of the room. At any other time such
behaviour would have been severely punished, but at the
time Mother scarcely had eyes for anyone but Sasha.

'Good heavens, what's the matter with her?' was all she
said as she jerked her hand away. 'What a little wildcat she's
growing into!'

Although Sasha went on sleeping all day, Mother calmed
down a little. At a family council it was decided to shut the
shutters in her room and let her sleep. When it grew dusk a
candle was brought in and an attempt was made to wake her
up and get her to eat something. She roused herself, drank a
glass of milk, and went off to sleep again. The next day the
same thing happened, and Mother began to worry.

'There's nothing really wrong with her,' said Nanny, who
had not moved from Sasha's bedside. 'It's the anxiety that wore
her out and all that worrying that she would never study.'

Indeed, Sasha was sleeping quite peacefully; and at last
opened her eyes.

'Darling,' said Mother kissing her tenderly, 'we can't let
you fall asleep again. You really mustn't, Sasha!'

Sasha lifted herself up in bed with difficulty. Her eyes were
still closed, but she was obviously trying to keep awake.

'We'll pour some cold water over you and that'll get rid

41

of your sleep,' announced Mother. The sick girl, supported on both sides as she was still too weak to walk unaided, was led out into the main hall. Buckets of cold water were poured over her, she was rubbed down, carried into the dining-room and laid on the sofa.

Though we had already had dinner we were ordered to sit round the table. Not daring to show our surprise we took our usual places and discussed the extraordinary things that were going on in whispers.

Eventually Mother announced that today we were celebrating the fact that Sasha was going to a *pensionnat* to study; and then Minodora entered the room carrying a coffee-pot and two jugs—one containing cream and the other clotted cream. We all loved coffee but had hardly ever had it since we had come down in the world; according to Mother it was too much of a luxury.

We pounced on the treat.

'Are we having one cup or two?' asked Zarya, noticing with horror that the bottom of his cup was visible already.

'Two cups, two,' answered Mother with a smile.

'This is nothing to what we shall be having,' murmured Nanny, more pleased than anyone to see the children enjoying themselves so much. 'This is the day we've been living for.' And as she spoke she poured coffee from her own cup into mine and Zarya's.

We had barely finished our coffee when Minodora brought in a tray of sponge-cakes with whipped cream, jam tarts, apples fresh from the garden, and little cucumbers steeped in honey. Zarya burst into a wild whinny of a laugh and I started wriggling on my chair. Nanny prodded us under the table in an attempt to remind us that Mother's wrath might break over our heads at any minute.

'Mother, darling,' Sasha begged her suddenly, 'do let me have just a tiny little sleep!'

Making the Estate Pay

'Darling, this is dreadful. . . . Do try to keep awake for an hour or so—here, have something to eat.'

'I don't want anything to eat. You could give me a present of two or three tarts if you like so that I could have them for my own and give them away to somebody if I wanted to.'

'Take what you like, darling,' said Mother. 'But what *can* we do to stop you feeling so sleepy?'

'There is one thing, but I'm afraid it might make you cross.'

It was a long time before Mother could persuade Sasha to tell her what it was, but eventually she admitted that she might not feel so much like sleeping if Vaska were allowed to play his violin to her.

Nanny found the solution while Mother was still making up her mind; a bed could be made up for Sasha in the side-wing, and Vaska could play there to his heart's content without disturbing Mother's after-dinner sleep.

'It's true I haven't been sleeping well the last few nights,' Mother admitted—and gave her consent.

So there the three of us were in the side-wing: Sasha in bed, Nanny knitting a sock, me making a shirt for a doll. When Vaska came in he put his violin on a chair, threw himself on his knees beside my sister and kissed her hand.

'Dear Miss Sasha,' he started. 'Oh, God, if only I could get work in a theatre!'

'Come along, Vaska,' said Sasha, giving him a sponge-cake and the tarts, 'eat these and then play something for me.'

'Oh, Miss Sasha, you are an angel. . . . But may I keep them for my wife?'

'Vaska, did you know, I'm going away to study! It all happened so suddenly, perhaps your luck will turn too,' said Sasha in an attempt to cheer him. 'Don't give up, now!'

'No, Miss, it's too late. I'll tell you a secret,' replied Vaska, lowering his voice. 'When your mother threatened to send me into the Army I wrote to the Prince. I reminded him that he had once wanted to buy me but that my old master had refused: things are quite different now, I said, and the mistress has decided to send me for a soldier because I'm no good at peasant's work, so perhaps you would be generous enough to buy me. I wrote to him about Minodora too; I can guarantee that my wife will please the princess, I said, for providence has given her the proper bearing for a chambermaid in the house of a nobleman . . . but would you believe it, Miss, two months have gone and there's been no answer. It's all up with me now, Miss—one day the mistress is going to lose patience with me and I'll be sent into the Army. And look at the insults I have to put up with! I do all the errands as well as can be but as soon as I have a spare moment the bailiff puts me to clean out the stables or cart manure, it's just done on purpose to humiliate me. And then there are the noises, Miss . . . noises, the whole time I hear noises everywhere and they're wearing me out. They're inside my head and my heart, they keep making little tunes and flourishes inside my head and my heart. Take today—as soon as I heard you were better and were going away the noises started a-hammering as if they were beating out a march to celebrate your recovery. I didn't dare touch my violin then and I don't know what it will sound like now, but if you listen I'll try.'

And Vaska took up his violin and began to play. Every now and then he explained what he was playing: 'Listen to this, little Missy,' he told me. 'Here are all God's creatures giving thanks that your sister is better. Now you can hear the birds twittering and the cuckoo calling; and here's the burble of a stream.'

He lowered his bow and for a few moments there was silence. Then, as if he had gathered his strength, he announced in trembling tones: 'And this is my own miserable fate.' What he played was terribly sad, the sort of thing I suppose the peasants used to mean when they talked about Vaska's 'howling'.

It made Sasha weep. 'Lord, Vaska, did you compose that yourself? Oh, God, why can't I do something for you? You're a genius, Vaska, a real genius,' she said.

In a few days Sasha was quite well again, totally pre-occupied with the thought of the *pensionnat*. She kept running to Nanny about it: Mother was out of the house as usual, and in any case she was always much more open with Nanny.

'Nanny, Nanny,' she would shout, running into our room. 'Suppose they find out I don't know anything? They can't put me in the first form at fourteen!'

Mother sent Nanny with letters to Mme Voinov and Olga Petrovna, her governess; she wanted to know if the governess could examine Sasha and give her some tuition if necessary. The answer could not have been better: Mme Voinov invited Sasha to stay and the governess was perfectly agreeable to giving her lessons after the children had gone to bed. In lieu of payment Olga Petrovna, who wanted to go to Vitebsk to see her sister, asked Mother to drive her there with Sasha and send horses for her again in three weeks' time. On her part she promised to recommend Sasha to all the *pensionnat* teachers, whom she knew quite well.

For the first time since Father's death the house rang with happy laughter, and on the following Sunday the whole family went to church. We stood out sharply from the rest of the congregation; the landowners' wives and families wore gay dresses but we formed a dark cloud to one side of them. After the fashion of the times our black frocks were trimmed as a sign of mourning with bands of white material.

Mother and Nanny knelt in tears throughout the service. Even Sasha, who carried flowers in her hands, was kneeling; but catching sight of Olga Petrovna she got up and began quietly edging towards her. After the service Olga Petrovna told us we were all invited to the Voinovs' for dinner.

The Voinovs were very wealthy people: they had two estates, crowds of servants, a large house with numerous out-buildings, and round the house a beautiful but not over-large garden with avenues of trees, flower-beds and lakes. When we got there the two children, eight-year-old Olga and Mitya, who was seven, took us into the nursery. The sight of it staggered Zarya and me; we had never seen such toys—though this was hardly surprising, for since Father's death Mother had not spent a ha'penny on toys for us.

We were called to the table before Olga and Mitya had had time to show us all their treasures. Throughout the meal I sat with eyes wide open looking at the unfamiliar dishes and the beautiful china and silver; but most of all I was fascinated by our host.

There was something of both the owl and the monkey about Peter Petrovitch Voinov. On his thin body sat a tiny ball of a head like the head of an owl. His reddish hair, cut *en brosse*, stuck up, and even his face was covered with a shorter, sparser variety of it; but most alarming of all was the expression in his piercing eyes, which bored into you like those of a bird of prey. I must have stared at him with my mouth open, because Mother pulled my hand angrily and told me to look at my plate instead of gazing about.

After dinner our host got up and went to have a nap in his study. We children went into the garden with Nanny, and Mother settled down in the summer-house with Nyuta and Mme Voinov. This was the solemn moment when Olga Petrovna was examining Sasha in the nursery.

When we had had enough running about the garden and playing we went back indoors. Mme Voinov was already pouring out tea behind a round table; luckily for us, this time the host was not there. Olga Petrovna and Sasha were still absent.

Making the Estate Pay

Then the door opened and they came in. Nanny, who was standing behind my chair, took one look at Sasha's face and realized that everything was all right; before Olga Petrovna had the chance to say a word, she turned towards the icons and began to cross herself, saying: 'Praise be to Thee, O Lord, that Thou hast listened to the prayers of Thy servant!'

This was greeted by general laughter, but Olga Petrovna told her: 'You really have got something to be pleased about, Nanny—your Sasha is beautifully prepared: such a good memory, and so well-read!' And she turned to Mother and went on singing Sasha's praises.

The preparations took several weeks. All our former maids were re-installed in the maids' room making dresses and underwear for Sasha, and the only one who took no part in the work was the one who was the reason for it. Sasha sat in her room, not taking her eyes off her books. However, the day of her departure came at last; as had been arranged, she was accompanied by Olga Petrovna and our former maid Dunyasha, who from now on was to look after Sasha at the *pensionnat*; it was the custom in those days for a nobleman's daughter to have her personal maid. They were of course driven by Vaska, who had instructions to make some business contacts with tradespeople in the town.

I was delighted when some ten days later we heard the sound of carriage-bells and a servant shouted that Vaska was back. Sasha had sent presents for everybody. Mother worked out that she must have spent her whole winter's pocket money on them—writing-paper for Mother, knitting wool for Nyuta, a doll's head and an enormous coloured biscuit for me, sweets for Zarya and a small icon and a handkerchief for Nanny, who kept kissing them.

Vaska described the *pensionnat* to us in detail and told us how pleased Sasha had been with everything, and then gave a full report of his business dealings in Vitebsk. Although he had hardly taken any produce with him—the carriage, skilfully adapted by him from an ordinary cart, had been crammed with luggage—he had managed to bring home a considerable sum of money.

'Now, Madam,' he said, 'when you send me to fetch Olga Petrovna the carriage will be empty and you must get as much produce ready as possible. I've made all sorts of contacts with the tradespeople in Vitebsk, and I swear to God I could sell the lot.'

'I'm very pleased with you, Vaska,' said Mother, graciously offering him her hand to kiss. 'You have done well.'

When he came back from Vitebsk the second time, having done still better, Mother could scarcely praise him enough. Her recent complaints about his uselessness forgotten, she began saying: 'He finds time for everything, you know—fetches water, chops wood, and when it comes to making a sale he has a positive gift for it—and that's more than you can say about his wretched music!'

But, surprisingly enough, Vaska's music did bring her an enormous profit in the end. This is what happened.

One day during the latter half of the winter Mother was told that a man had come to see her with a letter from Princess G., whose husband had employed Vaska in his orchestra. The Princess wrote that her husband, who had died recently, had at one time wanted to buy Vaska; he had considered him exceptionally gifted and had thought of giving him his freedom. My father's refusal had greatly disappointed the Prince, but in his memory the Princess had decided to carry out his wish and was now asking Mother to sell her Vaska together with his wife.

Mother, although in many respects she differed from her contemporaries, really could not comprehend how such a noble and wealthy woman as Princess G. could want to buy a serf merely to give him his freedom. She was aware that wealthy landowners did occasionally free a serf but it was usually in recognition of some outstanding service: but to buy a serf and then free him just so that he could develop his gift for music—that seemed downright ridiculous to her, and she dismissed it as an example of 'rich man's nonsense'. Being unwilling to part with Vaska and Minodora, to whom she had become attached during the past month, she asked fifteen hundred roubles for them in the firm belief that the Princess would never pay such a sum.

Several weeks passed. One wintry Sunday morning an empty carriage driven by two horses pulled up at the porch and the driver handed Mother a packet of money and a letter. Princess G. had not only sent all that Mother had asked but had added a few dozen roubles for incidental expenses connected with the drawing of the deeds.

Not only our family but the peasants as well were astonished by what had happened, and the news of Vaska's sale spread round the villages. The same day our yard was crowded with peasants and their women and children. No one could understand what was happening: Vaska was being bought for a ridiculous sum, being given his freedom, honoured by being sent for with a coachman and carriage instead of an ordinary peasant's cart—and all for strumming on a fiddle!

We all came out on to the front porch and immediately there was a solemn silence. Vaska crossed the yard, putting one foot in front of the other with reluctance. Behind him walked Minodora, wiping the tears from her face.

Vaska lurched over and fell at Mother's feet; by now she too was in tears. Then he knelt before Nanny and the rest of us in turn; he even bowed low to the crowd of peasants. The gesture touched them: although he had been bought for 'all that money' and driven away in splendour, Vaska, so far from putting on airs, had accepted his luck with humility and even bowed low to everybody.

'Heavens above,' said Nanny as she dried her tears, 'how sad he was to say good-bye—so sad it quite broke my heart. He seemed scarcely alive when they settled him into the carriage. It was hard for him to leave the nest, poor soul! You could see he was scared at the thought of going to the Princess.'

'What's the Princess to him now?' interrupted Mother. 'He's a Free Cossack, as the phrase goes.'

'That's what worries him, poor thing.'

'What do you mean?'

'Well, Madam, take this freedom. I look at it like this: he was a serf, that means he took orders—go and chop wood, run over to the smithy or the mill. . . . That went on all the time, and it means you don't have to worry your head with thinking or break your heart over some worry. Now of course he's free with no elders and betters to tell him what to do, and he'll have to work out everything for himself.'

'Really, Nanny,' cried Mother, unable to contain herself any longer, 'you're not a stupid woman, but you're talking absolute rubbish. How can you compare a serf with a free man?' But Nanny couldn't be persuaded.

Six months after Vaska's departure Sasha, in Vitebsk, had a letter from him. He had not forgotten his beloved 'Miss' who had always cheered him up in times of stress, and was writing to tell her that he and his wife now lived in Moscow: Minodora worked for the Princess as a maid, and received proper wages, and he himself played in an orchestra in one of the Moscow theatres.

A year later he wrote again, this time to say that the Princess was going abroad for good and that he and Minodora were going with her.

That was his last letter. What happened to him afterwards we never knew.

3

Serfs and Neighbours

Under Mother's management the condition of the estate improved all the time—thanks not only to her own unceasing efforts but also to Nanny's painstaking devotion. Without Nanny, Mother would never have become familiar with the minutest details of life in each one of the peasant households—for, in spite of her own straightforward attitude to them and the fact that she herself often went to see them in their homes, her people remained cold towards her. Nanny was treated quite differently; everywhere the peasants treated her as one of themselves, she was always invited to peasant weddings, and she had many godchildren among the village children. Nanny used to visit the sick and take them medicine and gifts such as white bread or a child's shirt made from some old thing of ours.

'But we're so poor now,' one of the peasants complained to her. 'The bread's made with chaff almost all the time now and right up to the end of summer there's nothing to cook but soup from nettles and sorrel, and this year there's not even any milk to thicken it because the last of the cows is dead.'

'The mistress is better than most, she doesn't beat us,' the woman Nanny was visiting would say, 'but that's the most you can say for her: it's herself she thinks of first, that's the sort she is. Come harvest and she's always under your heels the whole day making sure you aren't lacking work for a minute. She gives you no time to breathe. She kept on calling the other day and when I came up she said, "What's the matter, Anna? You keep running off somewhere.'

' "Mistress dear," I said, "I've a baby lying over by the bushes and I must go and feed him."

' "Well," she says, "and how old is he?"

' "Four months and a bit, Mistress, and won't take nothing but the breast."

' "Oh, feed him if you must," she says, "but don't waste time playing with him. I never had time to play with mine." '

'The Lord knows she was telling you the truth,' Nanny replied. 'She still has no time to play. Up at daybreak, she is. . . . But don't you worry about the cow, I'll beg one for you, just see if I don't.'

'You do your best, my dears, you do your best,' Nanny would tell the peasants. 'The late Master always looked after his serfs well and he had you on his mind even just before he died. As God's my witness the Mistress will do you no harm, she'll do as he wanted her to.'

'Tell us honestly,' a young peasant once asked her, 'what was it the Master said as he lay dying? I've heard tell he went for her, hard. "Don't you hurt the peasants," he said, "or they'll curse you and put a stake through your grave." '

'He never said anything about stakes,' Nanny told him, 'I swear before God he never said anything of the kind. The Mistress and I were standing at his bedside while he died and I remember all his words as if they were a prayer.'

I was a witness of all these conversations, for Nanny took me with her everywhere she went. After Nina's death she entrusted me to no one, and in any case I would not be parted from her. Sitting on a bench in a corner I used to listen wide-eyed.

'And how is Timofey the bailiff treating you?' Nanny might ask the peasants. 'I hear he's getting a bit free with his fists, and not too careful with the mistress's property. Is it true, do you know, or just gossip?'

Then she would go on: 'Who would you say was the best worker on the estate? Who do you think is the fairest-minded of all the peasants at Pogoreloye?'

Mother found such conversations immensely valuable. It was on our return from one of these visits that Nanny told her the bailiff Timofey was beginning to drink, and that the hardest-working and most reliable of the peasants was Louka.

Next Sunday she called him in to see her and after a long talk appointed him bailiff in Timofey's place.

The bailiff had his land worked by the peasants, and if his cottage or sheds needed repairs these, too, were done by Mother's workmen. On being given his job the bailiff was provided from his mistress's livestock with a cow and several sheep, and was given monthly amounts of rye, barley and buckwheat. He had no tithes to pay to the Big House, though in summer each peasant family had to produce set quantities of eggs, nuts and mushrooms for their mistress and in winter woven and spun material. The bailiff and his family were free of all these duties and he was the only peasant who could count in good years and bad on eating bread made without chaff and soup with some thickening in it.

Hard as our peasants' life might be they would have fared far worse on neighbouring estates.

Soon after we moved out into the country peasants from Bukhonovo started coming to see Mother. Bukhonovo belonged to Mother's elder brother Ivan Stepanovich Gonetsky, who lived in St. Petersburg, and the estate was managed by a German called Karl Karlovich. Before coming to see

Mother the peasants would beg Nanny to get Mother's protection for them and persuade her to put some curb on the activities of Karla, as they called him—but Mother told Nanny quite firmly she must send them away. She said that although she recognized the justice of their complaints there was nothing she could do as she had no right to interfere in her brother's business.

However, one day in spring a great crowd of peasants from Bukhonovo gathered outside our porch on a holiday. In spite of Mother's refusal to come out they would not go away and even said they would stay there until the mistress heard them out. Mother had to come out willy-nilly, whereupon several men stepped out of the crowd.

They complained about Karla at some length and gave Mother a detailed account of his vicious behaviour: what they wanted her to do was to come to Bukhonovo, see for herself, and then write to their master, her brother.

Mother heard them out and promised to do as they asked. The following Sunday she set out for Bukhonovo and Nanny and I went with her. Nanny could be relied on to make herself useful and my going was regarded as a little treat.

Mother had arranged that we should take our own food with us. 'This Karla will ask us to visit him,' she said, 'but I'm not prepared to enter his house. To eat a man's bread and then write a complaint about him isn't my way of doing things at all.'

The Big House at Bukhonovo stood on the other side of our lake. Mother decided to go over by boat and took the bailiff and two other peasants to row us over.

Karl Karlovich came up to us as we landed. He was a thick-set man of medium height with a slight paunch and a very white puffy face, with a high colour in his cheeks and blue eyes. He had extraordinarily protuberant red lips like leeches replete with blood.

Serfs and Neighbours

Karla greeted Mother with as pleased and gay an expression as if he were greeting his own mother and showered compliments upon her. His Russian was not perfect but despite an accent he was completely comprehensible; he had been meaning to visit Mother for a long time, he said, and was delighted to see her. 'There is a samovar and something to eat on the table,' he concluded.

Mother was an honest straightforward person who loathed every kind of pretence and deception. She said at once that she was unable to accept his invitation as she was not paying a social call but had come to inspect the peasants' living conditions in order to make a report to her brother.

Karla's expression altered when he heard this and his attitude changed immediately from subservience to abuse. He told Mother sharply that she had no right to make an inspection; he was in charge of the management of the estate, he said, and that meant he was the absolute and only master. He came closer and closer to Mother as he spoke and practically shouted the last words at her in his high-pitched voice.

Nanny raised her hands in horror. 'How dare you, you German sausage you!' she cried. 'How dare you talk to the mistress like that?'

'Have a care, you old witch,' shouted Karla, raising his stick in her direction.

I burst into tears, but there was nothing of the coward in Mother. She lifted her head proudly and told him angrily: 'Just you dare to touch any of my family or my peasants! Out of my way, I have my duty to do!' And with these words she moved resolutely forward, her little retinue following. This was so unexpected that Karla even backed a little, though he continued to shout threats at us.

Mother went into every hut. She asked each peasant whether he had a cow or a horse, how many days he had to work for the estate and what taxes he paid, whether he had been punished and if so for what. She ordered bread and soup to be brought her, tasted everything, examined the children, visited the stables and other outbuildings if there were any, and put down everything in a notebook. We spent the whole day inspecting the peasants at Bukhonovo, and as soon as she got home Mother sat down to write her brother a letter.

'Knowing your nobility of heart, dear brother, I trust that you will not leave Karla's wickedness unpunished but will put an end to his management which is so detrimental to your interests. I can prove that he has practically ruined your estate and, I dare to say, dishonoured your family name,' she concluded.

My Uncle Ivan had always dismissed reports of landowners ill-treating their peasants as fairy stories concocted by people with nothing better to do, so Mother's letter coming from the sister in whom he had implicit confidence impressed him enormously. What horrified him more than anything else, however, was the fact that his manager had put the family name under a cloud; he wrote that Mother should have told him about Karla's atrocities earlier and begged her to take over the management of the estate. He wrote separately to the German telling him to quit the estate immediately and to the authorities asking him to make sure there was no delay in his departure.

The state of affairs at Bukhonovo before Mother took over its management was not an isolated case.

Not far from our estate there was another smaller one belonging to three sisters called Tonchev of whom the youngest was nearly forty and the eldest getting on for fifty. The three lived together, were devoted to each other and called each other by pet names: Emily, the eldest, was 'Mila'; Concordia, the second, 'Dia'; and Eulampia, the third, 'Lala'. Among the neighbours the three of them went under the collective name of the Sweetie-bitches.

Serfs and Neighbours

If Mila had put on military uniform no one would ever have guessed it was a woman dressed up. Tall and scraggy and thin, she had long arms, enormous feet and a voice as deep as a man's: she always went about with a stick in her hands and a huge dog ready at her orders to attack a man, rip his clothes and savage him severely.

The second sister was reminiscent of a rag doll; she was fat and flabby with somewhat indistinct features. Her forehead, nose and cheeks looked unnaturally red as though the skin had been scraped from her face.

In contrast to Mila's stentorian tones Dia wriggled about and shut her eyes as she talked; she adopted an artificially dulcet way of speaking though her natural voice was as creaky as a rusting hinge.

Although Lala, the third sister, was slightly more presentable than her elder sisters, her way of behaving seemed almost the oddest. In spite of her forty years Lala carried on as naïvely as a girl, making eyes at every man and acting like a mischievous child who cannot keep still.

Lala was the favourite; her sisters considered her a beauty, dressed her up, spoiled her and never gave up hope of seeing her married. With Lala's dowry constantly in mind, they tortured their serfs by keeping them at the embroidery frames and looms day and night. The peasants who belonged to the Tonchevs not only had a heavier 'master's duty' than was done on other estates, but if the weather was good and Mila's hay not cut they had to work even on 'peasants' days'. This apart, the women had very heavy duties both summer and winter: each had to provide for Lala's dowry a set amount of linen, had to weave with cotton thread and wool, and had to embroider towels and sheets. In the summer loads of berries and mushrooms had to be gathered for the sisters— and in fact the peasants were so busy all the year round that they had no time left for their own work. Hardly a day passed without somebody being thrashed by way of punishment: for the smallest fault, offending peasants were mercilessly beaten by the bailiff in the presence of the two elder sisters. The Tonchevs themselves smacked their maids' cheeks so often they continuously went about with swollen faces.

On more than one occasion the peasants came to their mistress complaining that they were suffering not only from poverty but from lice, as the women had time neither to make linen for shirts nor even to wash them; but Mila's hard heart could not be softened. When the peasants realized this, there were outbreaks of downright disobedience and some of them ran away.

Things came to a head in an incident which took place in early autumn when the sisters were on their way home from a name-day party. They were driving in a carriage with a coachman; it was about midnight and very dark, and they had some three miles of forest to cross. After about a mile they were surrounded by a crowd of people; some took the horses by the reins and pulled down the coachman and others pulled the sisters, half-dead with fright, from their carriage. Lala and the coachman were tied up, gagged, and dragged to the side of the road and Mila and Dia were severely thrashed.

There was no hope of identifying the assailants because their heads were covered in sacks with holes cut for eyes. They had even put nuts or dried peas in their mouths so that the few words spoken during the attack should not give them away.

They all vanished into the forest, leaving their astonished victims unable to shout; but at last the youngest managed to free her mouth from the gag and she began to call for help. For a long time her cries went unanswered but eventually a landowner, returning home from the party the sisters had been to, heard their shouts and hastened to the rescue. It was only thanks to him that the sisters did not have to spend the night in the forest.

A few months after this incident the sisters' newly-completed house was burned to the ground. They had already reached the packing stage, preparatory to moving in, when they heard the news. This time there was plenty of evidence, but the man who had set fire to the house ran away that same night and was never discovered.

Life on the estate was dull, and it was only at the Voinovs' that I could play to my heart's content. I became very friendly with the young children, Olga and Mitya; had it not been for them, I should never have known the laughter and chatter of noise of the real games of childhood. Having run about until we nearly dropped, we would be given picture-books from France and Olga Petrovna would read us a story; the other children laughed happily but, not knowing a word of French, I used to turn scarlet with shame and my eyes would fill with tears. Olga Petrovna would immediately begin to explain the story in Russian or get the cards out or fetch a box of dolls. However, we preferred fairy tales to any game and it was here that I took the limelight.

I had picked up many stories from Nanny, Sasha and the maids, and often when I re-told them I would alter the endings or invent various additional adventures. These tales I considered my own, and Olga and Mitya listened to them enraptured; when the adults heard about the stories I 'made up', they too wanted to hear them. Despite my shyness I began to include them in my audience, whose close attention combined with adult praise went to my head.

'If the others show off their wealth and knowledge of French in front of me', I said to myself, 'I shall have to show them what I can do when it comes to stories.'

Back at home I continually pondered how to invent even more startling tales for my friends, and so began to include in them monsters, werewolves, cannibals and other horrors. I acted out my tales as I told them; speaking in graveyard tones, raising and lowering my voice, roaring and screaming, banging a stick on the floor, and running about on all fours to imitate animals. Mitya and Olga were so entranced by my stories that they would demand one as soon as they saw me and we gave up playing games altogether. Mitya was prepared to listen from morning till night, though he shook like a leaf in the more frightening places. If I stopped he would tearfully beg me to continue; it worried me when he cried, and I tried to calm him down by offering to leave out the worst bits, but he always said: 'No, don't miss out *anything*, I want to hear all the horrid things.'

My stories usually ended in us all howling. When the grown-ups came into the room and discovered the reason they usually roared with laughter instead of making any attempt to stop my pernicious tales.

If Voinov were away from home we would go into his study, though it was difficult to think of the room as such. It was almost filled with embroidery frames and might have been taken for a maid's room but for a desk in one corner. Voinov, with his round owlish eyes and hunched-up simian figure, was very fond of embroidering—but combined this feminine trait with a brutality for which he was famous. Serfs old and young feared him like the plague and he punished them severely for the slightest offence. He would sit calmly at his embroidery frame, working coloured silks on to flounces for his wife's dresses, while groans and screams of peasants being thrashed in the barn came through the open window of his study. His wife—young, beautiful, well educated and kind—was the exact opposite of her husband. Like my mother, she knew hardly any of the neighbours, and the only family with whom she was on friendly terms was ours.

When the Voinov children were due to visit us for the first time I was very worried by the fact that I had no toys—but as usual Nanny came to the rescue. She brought several hampers containing our old theatrical costumes down from the attic and, though everything that was really any good had already been used up, she and Nyuta began to sort out the remnants and started sewing and contriving until they had made something of it.

As soon as the Voinovs arrived, Nanny and Nyuta and Olga Petrovna dressed us up in various costumes with muslin skirts and crowns made of gold paper. First we showed ourselves to the grown-ups and then ran out into the yard where the peasants, old and young, rushed out of their huts to see us. We revelled in their astonishment as they stared in amazement and then came up to touch our dresses with their hands.

Although I always thoroughly enjoyed meeting the Voinov children, visiting the estate of my godfather, who lived about five miles away, was even more of a treat. Usually Nanny and I went over to see him in the morning and returned the same evening.

The moment we entered his house a wonderful wave of the scent with which his furniture and every corner of every room were permeated came wafting towards us. My godfather had a real passion for perfume, and it was not for nothing that the serfs nicknamed him the 'Scented Master'.

His daughters, who at that time lived in the town, were well aware of his passion and always sent him perfumed presents on his name-day and at the New Year—perhaps a magnificent box containing bottles of scent or a case with cut-glass bottles of eau-de-Cologne, boxes of differently-scented soap, bundles of perfumed candles or aromatic spills.

His underwear, outer garments and all his personal possessions were strongly perfumed, and little cushions and sachets of scented powder lay in every cupboard and chest of drawers.

'How delightful to see you, my dear visitors!' my god-father would greet Nanny and me in his hospitable way. 'Why is it that you visit me so rarely?'

'You spoil Liza quite enough as it is,' Nanny would tell him. 'She's quite lost her head and does nothing but dream of her next visit to you.'

'Well,' he would reply, 'we can't help being fond of each other, we have so much in common. The godfather likes scent and so does the god-daughter; godfather is interested in pigeons and his daughter is far from bored by them——' And I would throw myself on his neck with a shout of joy, kiss him, and run to inspect all the rooms. It was the bedroom which interested me most of all, and I always rushed first to his dressing-table which was covered with embroidered Russian linen. On it stood several crystal bowls containing various brushes, a manicure set and soaps of different scents and colours. When I had inspected and sniffed at every cake of soap I would run back to my godfather, sit down beside him, and snatch his gold snuff-box. It was encrusted with pretty stones and tightly shut: although I never opened it for fear of spilling the snuff, my hands would smell for some time afterwards of scent and fine snuff merely from having handled it.

Before we had been with him very long two round tables would be set in the dining-room. One was covered with things to eat—salted and pickled mushrooms, fish, cold pork, and a sucking pig standing on four legs in the middle as if it were still alive. The other table was laid for three people. Godfather kept an experienced chef who could not only cook but could also garnish his dishes attractively.

He spent all the profit accruing from his estate on himself, and since he had no extravagant tastes and lived alone, he could naturally afford the best.

Knowing the love and respect with which Nanny was treated in our family, my godfather treated her as an equal, sitting her at the table and conversing with her for long periods on all sorts of subjects. Nanny felt completely at home with him and talked freely and naturally about everything.

After dinner I would ask my godfather to show me his pigeons. He was very fond of his birds, and there were several dove-cotes in the yard though by now they were un-tenanted; too old to climb ladders, he had them moved into a special one-roomed hut in the middle of which was a biggish tree with peeling bark and plenty of branches. Shelves for nests had been put up round the walls and in a corner of the sand-strewn floor stood trays of grain and shallow troughs of water. Everything was kept in perfect order, and there was a special woman who looked after the pigeons.

When we entered the hut I used to be momentarily stunned by the cooing and the beating of wings. My godfather would sit on a bench and beckon the pigeons to him, and they would come and settle on his head and shoulders and run about on his lap. When we left the hut and went into the garden the pigeons would come too; the garden, though small, was my godfather's special pride. Here, under his guidance, a village lad who had learned his trade from a good gardener grew only flowers that were strongly scented—and in the spring when they were in bloom the garden would perfume the whole estate.

My godfather had another passion as well as perfume, pigeons and flowers: he collected coffins, which were housed in a barn specially allocated to them.

We heard the story of his strange collection from my godfather himself. At the age of fifty or so he fell ill and dreamed a curious dream. It was that he had suddenly died and that the carpenter, one of his serfs, had taken his measurements for a coffin—and then got drunk, lost the measurements, and botched up the coffin from memory. It turned out to be too short: my godfather had to be forced into it until his bones were breaking and, although he was dead, the pain was excruciating. . . .

The dream made such an impression on him that when he recovered he decided that a suitable coffin ought to be got ready for him while he was still alive. He went to the lengths of having his carpenter sent to Moscow to be trained; as soon as he had mastered the craft, the preparation of coffins began. My godfather was not satisfied with a single specimen, but had them built by the dozen. Some developed cracks after a few years, some fell to pieces, and others did not come up to his requirements; these last were presented to serfs in whose families there had been a death. Constantly preoccupied with the subject, my godfather gradually began to experiment with the material and outward appearance of his coffins. At first, being tall and thin, he stuck to long narrow ones—but then he heard about a sufferer from dropsy whose body swelled up to nearly twice its size when he died, and about a very tall man left quite small after a prolonged and severe illness. After this my godfather began to order coffins suitable for bodies of all sorts of shapes and sizes.

Dry straw was kept in all the coffins, and my godfather thought nothing of lying in each in turn just to show Nanny and me how comfortable he would be when he died. One day, however, he told us with regret that he now had to keep the barn very carefully locked. A day or two previously a group of young men had been passing his house in a somewhat convivial state and decided it would be a good place to stay the night. As it was already past twelve they did not want to bother their host and, leaving their coachmen to look after their horses and carriages in the yard, they settled down for the night in the barn. The coffins, being filled with straw, made good beds.

When my godfather entered the barn quite unsuspectingly the next morning tousled heads suddenly emerged from all the coffins. He was scared stiff at first and then, when he realized what had happened, so furious that for the first time in his life he broke the laws of hospitality and offered his guests neither a drink of tea nor anything to eat.

'Just imagine, my dear!' he told Nanny. 'Nothing is sacred to them. They eat and drink themselves silly and then clamber into my coffins with mud on their boots and their clothes reeking of wine. They have desecrated all that is holy to me!'

On yet another estate not far from ours there lived an uncle of mine, my late father's brother Maxim Grigoryevich Tsevlovsky. Uncle Max, as we called him, was the most notorious woman-hater in the district—not that he always had been; before the deplorable incident which altered his whole life he had been renowned as a man who spent money freely, lived a gay life and enjoyed feminine company. He had lived mostly in St. Petersburg and only visited his estate in the summer, and then never for very long. Here he rested from the hectic life of the capital and arranged his 'business affairs'—disposing of a section of forest for timber, selling a few serfs, letting his neighbours buy his corn cheap and in fact raising the money for his winter in town.

Then, suddenly, this sophisticated man fell madly in love with one of his neighbours' serfs, a girl called Varya. She could read and write and had acquired a certain polish while acting as maid to the daughter of her master. Uncle Max bought Varya without hesitation and took her to his modest

E

country house; but, however great his devotion, he had no wish to marry her even when a daughter was born to them. The most Varya could extract from him was freedom for her little girl.

The *affaire* caused a great scandal at the time and most of the neighbours refused to have anything to do with Uncle Max and his family. Once or twice a year Varya returned to the estate of her former master to see her relatives, and coming home one day after a brief absence Uncle Max could find neither Varya nor his small daughter—only a letter reproaching him for refusing Varya's request that she and her daughter should bear his name. Since he seemed ashamed to be her husband she had decided to leave him for another man, whom she would have married by the time he received her letter.

When he read what she had written Uncle Max roared with fury like a wounded animal and had a seizure; spasms contorted his face and body, and he trembled and shuddered as in a fever. He never completely recovered from the stroke and spent the rest of his life indoors. Sometimes he even found it difficult to walk and stayed for the best part of the day by his window in an arm-chair. No woman apart from my mother was allowed across his threshold; he even refused to see us nieces for a long time, but he was very fond of my brother Zarya, who was his godson, and was always genuinely delighted when Zarya came to see him.

One day, however, Uncle Max did ask Mother to bring his nieces over to see him. Knowing his dislike of feminine company she was very surprised; but, not wanting to irritate a sick man with a lot of questions, accepted his invitation with the sole comment that she was sorry he would miss seeing Sasha. Told of Sasha's passion for education, Uncle Max shrugged his shoulders and said he was surprised Mother did not realize how much harm she was doing Sasha by encouraging her in her desire to study. All women, according to him, were mean deceitful creatures sent as a curse from heaven; but women who were not only intelligent but educated were a positive menace.

Contrary to our expectations Uncle Max greeted us very kindly—though my first impression of him was decidedly unpleasant. He appeared before us like a living skeleton—head nearly bald, bony hands shaking, face lined with deep furrows and, nastiest of all, a permanent sneer at the corners of his thin lips.

We had barely had time to greet him when a manservant began to serve us with food. Nanny was going to stand behind my chair, but Uncle Max protested: 'All the ladies are dining with me today,' he said, 'and in any case you always sit at table with the family at home.'

There were many courses and it was a good hour before we laid down our spoons and forks; the dessert was particularly rich. When at last we stopped chewing and nibbling, the manservant placed on the table a tray on which were various boxes and lengths of material. Uncle Max watched us carefully as he handed them out, showering all of us with presents.

Nanny and Nyuta thanked him with polite restraint, but each new gift made me more excited: I threw myself on my uncle's neck and kissed him, and ran chattering delightedly between Nanny and my sister to show them each piece of material and tell them what a pretty frock it would make. Then Uncle Max pushed a case containing gold ear-rings over to Nyuta and to me a box full of rings, beads and coloured ribbons. He told Nanny to put them all on me and show me a mirror: and when I saw myself all decked up in them I went mad, jumping and screaming with joy and continually kissing my uncle.

So ended our first visit to him, but before the week was

out he sent us another invitation. This time we got ourselves ready without so much apprehension—on the contrary, I kept urging Nanny to dress herself quickly, and we set off with hearts beating in anticipation.

This time the dinner was just as magnificent and the dessert just as rich, but I hurried through it unappreciatively, awaiting with impatience the arrival of the manservant with the present. However, dinner came to an end and no splendid tray appeared. When Uncle Max suggested we might leave the table I could not restrain my impatience and asked calmly: 'What about our presents?'

Uncle Max roared with laughter and said that this time there were none. My face must have fallen because he sat down beside me and asked me slyly: 'Tell me, were you really very frightened of the old ogre the first time you saw your uncle, and then did the ribbons and rings make you forget what a monster he is?'

Not suspecting the question was a trap, I answered frankly: 'Yes, they did. . . . The presents were nice: why aren't there any today?'

Nanny pulled at my sleeve and I looked up to see Nyuta's scared expression, but it was too late. Uncle Max threw himself back in his chair and roared again; the whole of his ungainly body shook and his face turned a deep red. His terrible laugh must have echoed right round the house, because the manservant and chef—still in white apron and hat —appeared in the doorway. Lifting up the chair in which the old man was still convulsed with laughter, they carried him up to his bedroom. Nanny hurried us home without waiting for him to recover from his attack.

Mother told us that when she went to see Uncle Max after this second visit he explained that he had only wanted to see his nieces to find out whether they were as mercenary as the rest of our sex. He had hoped that we, being the children of two such unusual people as his brother and our Mother, might differ from other women; but unfortunately he now had proof positive that this was not the case. According to him, we already showed the characteristic feminine traits; Nyuta had acquired deceitfulness and hypocrisy, while I had made no secret of my greed, passion for money, vanity and natural wickedness. His words made Mother so furious that she jumped up and left him without saying good-bye.

I never saw him again after our disastrous visit, and when he died it turned out that he had indeed left the whole of his impoverished little estate to Zarya, and there was not a penny for us nieces.

In our district, particularly on the other side of the lake, there were many impoverished noblemen—mean and miserable creatures whose small houses stood very close to each other, separated only by kitchen gardens or narrow strips of land on which stood a shed or two or a rank crop of weeds. In front of their poor dwellings stretched a muddy foul-smelling street where there were always dogs running up and down, pigs ambling about or cattle being driven along from the fields.

Nearly all the houses were built on the same pattern—two rooms divided by a passage and a kitchen. On the right lived the master and on the left his serfs; although each household could boast only a few, their quarters were always cramped and dirty. They slept on the floor, on benches by the fire, and in wooden bunks. Hens, cats and dogs ran about the room; half the floor space would be taken up by a loom, and there would also be a handmill for grinding corn for flour, buckets, trunks, and two or three tables under which were baskets containing hens either hatching eggs or rearing chicks.

Firewood was piled in every corner and in the middle was

a burning brand fixed high enough to light the whole room.
It could not be claimed this was a convenient form of illu-
mination; the wood spluttered and threw burning sparks on
to the floor, and the brand was spent so quickly it was
constantly having to be replaced.

In the houses of these smallholders among the impoverished
nobility—as with the well-to-do landowners—lived an
assortment of relatives and hangers-on: an unmarried niece,
an elderly sister of the master or the mistress, or perhaps an
uncle who had wasted his own fortune. Both the masters and
their wretched relatives spent the entire day doing nothing.
Not one ever made his own bed or even dusted or tidied a
table. Rough, sometimes even illiterate people, they had this
constant refrain: 'I am of noble birth: to work would be
beneath my dignity.'

They never read, but then the only books in the house
would be the almanac and one for interpreting dreams. They
killed time by playing cards, gossiping and quarrelling: the
head of the household would berate his poor relations for
battening on him, and they in turn would bring up all the
humiliations they had ever suffered. Smallholders who lived
in close proximity to each other quarrelled continuously between themselves and often took their complaints to the
authorities. There were various reasons for their endless
squabbles: living so close to each other meant that nearly
every day a horse or a cow or a pig would wander into the
wrong patch of ground. The infuriated owner would rush
out of the house shouting at his serfs to deal with the unin-
vited guest: the poor animal might be beaten or injured in
being driven into the stables. Then a fierce battle between the
neighbours would begin.

Many quarrels broke out over dogs: each family possessed
one and sometimes several. Being half-starved, they were
always stealing things from other people's yards and biting

children. However, it is not really possible to list all the origins of disputes—quarrelling broke out on the slightest pretext and often there were furious fights in the middle of the street.

One of them I can remember quite vividly; two women who were neighbours took to hurling boiling water at each other. Both these self-styled members of the nobility were shouting so loudly that a big crowd gathered and the neighbours all joined in the fight without stopping to ask what it was all about: stones and lumps of wood were thrown, hair was torn and faces were scratched. Attracted by the appalling noise—the fighters were shouting and screaming and the dogs were barking—more and more people ran out into the street. Relatives and friends armed with sticks, pokers and frying-pans rushed to the support of each side and the fight turned into a pitched battle. Sticks and pokers went flying through the air and the affair might have ended disastrously had not two old men had the happy idea of getting their serfs to fill buckets with water from the well and then empty it over the fighters.

The well-to-do landowner only tolerated his impoverished neighbour if he were bored or lonely. The smallholder would enter the study and sit on the edge of a chair, ready to jump up as soon as a more important visitor arrived. Should he not do so, his host would comment: 'What's the matter? You're behaving like a visitor!' The rich never hesitated to show how much they despised the poor and took every opportunity to enjoy a joke at their expense. Women were always insultingly referred to by their patronymics—Maria Petrovna as Petrovna, Anna Ivanovna as Ivanovna—and surnames twisted for comic effect.

Any smallholder who turned up to congratulate a rich landowner on his name-day or at some holiday was not served at his host's table but given something to eat in a side-

room or in the children's quarters, though sometimes an
extra place might be laid for him if he could be made to look
a clown or provide amusement for the guests. The host might
prompt him with: 'Well, tell us how it was you came to eat
herrings with the Tsar!'

'I did, you know, as true as I'm sitting here now,' the man
would begin. 'It's amazing, the way it happened. I was in
St. Petersburg on business at the time, and I happened to be
passing the palace when I caught sight of a gentleman standing by a window. You could have knocked me down with a
feather when I realized who it was—the Tsar himself, looking
the dead spit of his portraits. When I made so bold as to
take a second look, His Majesty beckoned me. . . . What
could I do? There were soldiers everywhere, but I made for
the way in. "The Emperor beckoned to me," I told them.
"What do you think I ought to do about it?"

' "Well," they said, "we shall have to let the chiefs of staff
know at once," they said, "and in the meanwhile you can
wait in the hall." So I went in and had a look round. My
godfathers, what a hall! Covered in mirrors all the way
round, it was. . . . Well, now, I was standing there in a state
of suspended animation when suddenly the door opened and
masses of generals all covered with medals marched up to me.
One of them, the chief one, he said to me: "Do you really
imagine it is possible to see the Emperor like this? Why,
everyone would want to." I gave him a most respectful bow,
but dignified, you know, like a nobleman should be, that is
to say I didn't bow *too* low: "Your Excellency," I said, "His
Majesty beckoned to me with his own hand—what was I to
do?"

'My generals began to fidget and whisper and finally one
said "Come this way". I went along with generals in front
of me, generals to the sides of me, generals behind me—
nothing but generals. All their chests were dripping with

medals. And the apartments we went through—my goodness, not a thing was missing. One room was encrusted with
diamonds, another plated with gold. . . . My head began to
spin and I didn't know whether I was on my head or my
heels. At last we arrived; the Tsar rose and cried sternly:
"What sort of person are you? Where are you from and
what do you want?"

' "Your Majesty," I said, "I am a nobleman from Smo-
lensk."

' "Ah, that's another story," said the Tsar. "Sit down, you
must be my guest. We'll have breakfast together." And,
goodness me, what a meal we head! But the herrings were
best, they simply melted in your mouth.'

This idiotic tale, which I heard myself several times, always
produced roars of appreciation from the audience; the landowners choked with laughter, roaring at every word and
clapping their hands.

One of the noble smallholders, Makrina Prokovyeva, was a
frequent visitor to our house. Makrina, as everybody called her
behind her back and some even to her face, lived apart from
the other smallholders and was our nearest neighbour. Over
forty (and looking much older), Makrina lived in the village
with her only daughter Zenya, a girl of fourteen or so.

She had very little land but it included a wonderful
orchard and a small farm with a few cattle, two or three
horses and some farmyard fowls. Makrina's house, like those
of the other smallholders, was divided into two: one half had
practically fallen down, and here were the servants' quarters,
heaps of junk and her store of potatoes. The other half consisted of a kitchen and two rooms occupied by mother and
daughter. In the bedroom stood two vast wooden beds big
enough to sleep several people both crosswise and lengthways.
Heaped high with feather mattresses and pillows, they needed
a stool before you could climb on to them.

Makrina's only two serfs were husband and wife—Terenty, who was called Tereshka, and Efimiya, or Fishka. They were hard workers and each would help the other, spending much of their time on the orchard. Its various fruit trees and bushes made it the best in the district and, as Makrina's holding did not produce enough corn and hay for her family, serfs and livestock, she had to barter her fruit. Makrina sold cherries, apples, pears, gooseberries, plums and raspberries—or, more often, exchanged them with her neighbours for barley, oats, hay or straw.

As well as the orchard, Tereshka had to manage with Fishka the kitchen garden and livestock. Had Makrina and her daughter been prepared to do any of the household work themselves, the serfs might have been able to cope with the rest of the property; but the mistress piled on to them all the jobs about the house as well. Tereshka acted as coachman, errand boy, carpenter, bricklayer, farmhand and gardener; while Fishka, apart from her outdoor work which included milking and seeing to the dairy produce, was cook, house-maid, washer-up and, on top of everything else, was constantly being interrupted to do footling little jobs.

If Zenya happened to drop a ball of wool while she was knitting, Makrina would lean out of the window and shout: 'Fishka, come here and find Miss Zenya's wool for her!'

'You come and milk the cows for me,' Fishka would shout back, 'and I'll pick up your silly ball of wool from under your nose.'

Makrina could not let this pass and ran out to the yard to slap the woman's face for being rude.

When Makrina ran up to her Fishka calmly pushed her aside with one hand and said: 'Don't you lay your hands on me! I've toothache as it is and if I have anything else to put up with I'll just lie down, and I shan't get up and you'll have to do all the work yourself·if you want anything to eat and drink.'

Unable to contain herself, Makrina started stamping her feet and cursing at Fishka—who, tall, strong and robust, took no notice whatever of her fat little mistress running round her like a small and infuriated dog. She just went on with what she was doing although the moment she bent down for anything Makrina ran up behind her and pounded on her back with her fists.

'All right, all right,' Fishka would say as if she hadn't felt a thing. 'You've had your way and that'll do. Now for the Lord's sake get back to your room, there's nothing you can do here and you only get in my way.'

Fishka's husband used to infuriate Makrina even more.

'Tereshka, come here at once: the table's fallen over and I want it put right," the high-born lady would shout from the window.

'What of it? I've got to get the harness off this horse, he's been sweating—you can't expect me to run your silly errands now': and he stayed where he was and went on unharnessing the horse.

'How dare you argue with me?' screamed Makrina.

'I'm busy,' answered Tereshka. 'I'll come and attend to you when I've finished what I'm doing.'

4

Nanny's Last Illness

So began our fifth year of life in the country. Zarya was sent to the Military College at Novgorod, and with Andrei at St. Petersburg and Sasha in a *pensionnat* at Vitebsk, the family was smaller. In our big country house there were only four of us left—Mother, Nyuta, Nanny and myself.

Nanny, we suddenly realized that spring, was growing thinner every day. Mother was very worried over what to do; fetching the doctor from town was very difficult and expensive. Four journeys were involved, which meant a man and horses off work for five or six days—and as the doctor would be away from his practice for so long he would expect a large fee.

Just then, however, Mme Voinov fell ill and her husband sent horses into town for the doctor. They sent word through their governess suggesting that Mother might like to take advantage of his visit.

Nanny's pale cheeks flushed when she heard of the Voinovs' offer, but Mother would not let her say a word. 'Don't forget,' she said, 'that if anything happens to you it'll be the end of both my children and my estate.'

She took Nanny over to the Voinovs without further discussion. The doctor could find nothing serious but advised two or three months' rest, so it was decided that Nanny should go to Kiev on a pilgrimage.

I was in despair at the news that Nanny would be going away, and when I thought of the forthcoming parting I either cried or sat for hours in the same place refusing to answer even Nanny's questions. Mother and Nyuta scolded me and tried to shame me but it made no difference, I only grew more and more miserable; once I even cried so hard in my sleep that I roused the whole household. I woke up to find Mother and Nanny at my bedside; they gave me something to drink and I calmed down. Nanny must have thought I had dropped off to sleep, for she said to Mother: 'You can do what you like, but I shan't go.'

The words had such an effect on me that I went calmly to sleep and got up in the morning completely recovered from my fit of depression.

A day or two later, however, I noticed that Nanny was behaving strangely; she would turn away from me as if embarrassed, her hands trembled and she didn't seem to want to talk to me. Suddenly we heard the Voinovs' voices at the door and I jumped happily up and ran to meet them. After half an hour Mother told me to get dressed immediately as I was going with them, and I was hurried into my coat.

A dreadful suspicion came into my head. I looked at Nanny: there was no doubt. Hurriedly she wiped away her tears and left the room. Calling out, I ran after her, but Mother grimly clutched my hand and dragged me back into the room.

Once at the Voinovs' the mistress of the house and the governess did everything they could to keep us entertained. We played in the garden, went rowing on the lake, read books and played with dolls. During the day I had no time to think about home and did not even remember Nanny and her going; but it was a long time before I could get to sleep that night, and I felt very lonely.

In those days there was no general conscription and noble-men and merchants were not obliged to do military service, but when a recruiting campaign was announced the land-owners had to provide a certain number of conscript soldiers from among their peasants. Many landowners took the oppor-tunity to get rid of men guilty of some offence, though in cases where a serf had been particularly tiresome his owner sent him to the Military Authorities, who would in turn issue a receipt, without waiting for the conscription. Call up was for twenty-five years but those with any sort of bad record remained soldiers for life.

A new conscript was bound hand and foot, shackled, and placed in a special hut to prevent him running away or com-mitting suicide. A few peasants always spent the night with him and early the next morning he was driven to the recruit-ing office in town. There was no sleep for the guards on such occasions; in spite of the poor wretch being tied up they were afraid that his family might help him to escape. Sleep was additionally impossible because the crying and keening of his relatives could be heard all night round the hut in which the recruit was being guarded.

The poor conscript's wife knew that she had nothing left to live for; there was nowhere for her to go but her husband's family's house, where for her keep the 'soldier's wife', as she was immediately dubbed, paid with her labour. The heaviest work was piled on her and she had to endure her mother-in-law's tongue and the reproaches—and as often as not the beatings—of her husband's sisters. Having lost her only protector she either pined away from misery or took to drink.

One night I was woken up by dreadful screaming. I called Domna but there was no answer. When I felt her bed and realized she was not there, I threw on some clothes and ran

out into the yard; the door of the house had been left un-
locked.

It was dawn. I went toward the voices, and soon found
myself near the bath-house, which was surrounded by a
dense crowd; occasionally a light flared up inside and illumin-
ated the faces of those sitting in the bath-house or standing
outside. On the ground I saw a group of young girls, the
conscript's sisters, weeping and crying: 'Beloved brother,
why are you leaving us to fend for ourselves?' Beside them
sat two old people, the conscript's parents; the old man sat
staring at the bath-house window and miserably shaking his
head and the old woman, who had just had water poured
over her to bring her to her senses, was dripping wet all over
her head and shoulders. Obviously past crying, she was as
motionless as if she had been frozen and just sat staring
fixedly in front of her. Next to her in a truly pitiful state was
the conscript's young wife; her hair dishevelled, her face
swollen with tears, she wept continuously—now throwing
herself on the ground, now jumping up and running to the
door of the bath-house, where she begged repeatedly to be
let in.

Eventually the door opened and Louka the bailiff came out.
'All right, my dear,' he said with a sigh. 'You can go in, but
this must be the last time. The old people can see their son,
too.'

I slipped in after them, and at first was able to remain unnoticed. I looked at the guards sitting on the benches and at
the young woman sobbing at her husband's feet. Suddenly
Louka saw me.

'What are you doing here, Miss Liza?' he asked with a
shake of his head. 'Domna will be in trouble on your
account.'

At this moment she came running in; as she dragged me
home and put me to bed again she scolded me, but then she

ran off again. For a long time I lay with wide-open eyes, unable to sleep because of what I had seen; but suddenly such a noise of shouting broke out again in the yard that my heart missed a beat and I jumped out of bed again and ran outside.

A horse and cart stood ready in the yard, with the conscript and guards near by. The man's relatives were led up to him in turn; each kissed him three times on the cheeks and gave him a low bow of farewell. He answered in the same fashion and then, bowing once more to them all, climbed into the cart. Two peasants joined him and sat one on each side.

A few days later I was just getting up when I heard shouts of 'Nanny is back, Nanny is back!' I ran to her but could not say a word, only let her kiss me and hug me.

Nanny hardly gave herself time to take off her coat and tidy herself after her journey before she started firing questions at us. 'Tell me, Nyuta,' she asked my sister, 'is there any news from Sasha? What are Andrei and Zarya doing? Tell me, dear, what do they say in their letters?'

While Nyuta was trying in reply to pass on all our news at once, Nanny took my head in her hands, looking into my eyes and covering my face with kisses.

'Goodness gracious, Liza, what can be the matter with you? Why are you so thin and pale? Have you been ill or something?'

My sister said I was thin because I had pined for her so much. Then Mother came back from the fields and the kisses and questions and answers began all over again.

'I must say, if you are better it doesn't show much,' said Mother, looking closely at Nanny. But Nanny declared she felt perfectly well, and changed the subject by talking about the children again. Mother took letters from my brothers and sister from a drawer and began to read.

In the evening after supper when we were by ourselves she asked me to tell her everything that had happened to me since she went away. I readily described my stay with the Voinovs and said how unhappy I had been without her.

I told Nanny about the conscript's being taken away and what had happened the night before. She was both worried and surprised that Domna had dared leave me alone at night; then, seeing I was tired, she began hurrying me to bed.

Suddenly she said that it was high time I began to do some studying. 'You're no longer a baby,' she said: 'do you realize what Sasha is doing already? Young she may be, and still studying herself, but she's helping the family. That's what education, with the Lord's help, does for you. You're just as good as the others, and after you've studied a little you'll be in a better position to face life.'

Soon I was asleep. The next day was Sunday: Mother stayed at home and Nanny took the opportunity to talk to her about me, reminding her it was time I was given some lessons. 'God gave Sasha a good brain,' she said, 'but books did a lot for her as well.'

Mother was far from taking offence at being reminded of her responsibilities by Nanny, for she was well aware that she had made many mistakes in bringing up her children and that she was very late in starting my education.

'All right, you old busybody,' she told Nanny good-naturedly: 'but fancy fussing about like this before you've even had time to catch up on the sleep you lost on your journey!' But she was in complete agreement and decided that I should begin without delay.

Monday, Nanny decided the next day, was too busy a day for me to make a start; and Mother agreed. The next day Nyuta was asked to find an alphabet book and do a few letters and words with me every day. Nanny insisted on being present too so that she could see the method of teaching, and she asked Mother to spare me ten minutes or so each evening to see what I had learned.

A Russian Childhood

'It's only a little idea of mine about the best way to do it,' Nanny said as she presented Mother with her plan for my education, 'but if Nyuta could teach her a line or so and I made her repeat it, then you'd have nothing to do when we came to you in the evening but congratulate us.'

'I know, I know,' smiled Mother. 'You're simply arranging all this so that your precious Liza doesn't get a knock on the side of the head from my thimble! Well, Nyuta, I suppose we'd better do as our Director says.'

In those days the alphabet was taught by giving a child groups of letters, which he repeated at first one by one and then all together. Our ABC had four or five consonants in a line which were neither short words nor even syllables; 'MRGVY, TKPRY, ZDRVY,' I read, twisting my tongue. Pronouncing this nonsense was so hard that the perspiration used to pour down my face; and had it not been for the fear of upsetting Nanny I'm sure I should have got stuck over these tongue-twisters. This often happened among the children of our neighbours; after struggling with the alphabet in vain for some time they lost all interest in learning and relapsed into illiteracy.

Each evening Nanny waited for Mother to return and then dragged me along so that she could go over my work. As I managed to learn the syllables by heart and read them off quickly, Mother always let me go in peace.

Sometimes after the lesson Nanny would begin to philosophize. 'This is all so difficult for a child. Why is all this tongue-twisting necessary? It seems so much simpler to make up a proper word, say "book" or "chair", then the child would soon pick up a great many words and before long he would be reading a book.'

'I'm afraid those who write books are cleverer than you and me,' Mother would retort—not realizing that Nanny had hit the nail on the head by the exercise of inherent common sense.

Nanny's Last Illness

When, after a considerable effort and with much reluctance, I had eventually mastered the detested ABC book, they began to teach me to write; and for reading I was given a History of the Church. Having stumbled through the first few pages, I began, much to Nanny's delight, to read fairly fluently.

Eventually it was decided to launch me into new subjects; my sister was to teach me arithmetic and my Mother French. This put a cruel strain on me, because Mother was rarely free until after supper, that is not before nine or ten at night, by which time she was exhausted; so she decided to give me my lessons in the morning. Actually you could hardly call it morning: Mother rose at dawn and left the house at six, so she said I was to be called at four. She had no other free time, but this enabled her to give me two hours without being late for work.

On the first day Nanny could not wake me up. Mother lost her patience, came in, and pulled at my arm until I tumbled out on to the floor, whereupon she told Nanny to pour a jug of cold water over my head and give me a brisk rub down. As I dressed Mother stood over me and read me a lecture: 'The luxuries of life are not for us. I too would much rather stay in bed. It is very pleasant to throw on a soft *peignoir* in the morning and lie down on a couch to drink hot coffee with cream off a silver tray, but unfortunately the Lord did not bless us with riches. You should be grateful to him that you have someone to teach you even at night.'

From then on I was roused at four in the morning whether it was frosty or mild, and each time I was drenched in cold water from head to foot. There was nothing to prevent me from going back to bed when the lesson was over, but I could never get to sleep again; and the whole day I went about feeling tired and miserable.

I had to dress quickly after my cold shower, not to get

warm but so as not to waste Mother's time. The result was that I dragged my clothes on anyhow, shivering partly from cold and the early hour but also with apprehension at the lesson which was to follow. Naturally I never had time to do my hair and it was always falling over my forehead and into my eyes. Mother used to pull it if I couldn't follow anything she said—so hard that I yelled until the whole household heard me. This made her even angrier and she pulled still harder, thrust me away, and smacked me over and over again. Sometimes she lost her temper so much that she would shout: 'Get over to the other table or I'll pull all your hair out by the roots!'

Mother had what Nanny called an easy-going nature, and it is true that since she herself quickly forgot any misdemeanour she never realized that other people might remember; when she came home in the evening she would speak to me pleasantly as though nothing had ever happened. Inside me, however, a feeling of hostility towards her was growing stronger and stronger; and when she entered a room I would run out and try to slip away somewhere rather than kiss her hand, as the custom was on meeting. Nanny, who always tried to soften my hard feelings against Mother, could make no impression on me now; as soon as she opened her mouth in Mother's defence I put my hands over my ears and threw myself on my bed to cry away my misery.

One day Mother was so cross with me during my lesson and shouted and smacked me and pulled my hair so much that I retreated into a stubborn silence. When she found she could not drag a single word out of me Mother jumped up in a fury and I don't know what she would have done to me had not Nanny rushed in and thrown herself at her feet in tears.

'Have pity on your child,' she cried. 'Perhaps the Lord did not give her a brain for French, perhaps she could manage without it.'

Nanny's Last Illness

Mother began shouting at Nanny and complaining she had spoiled me, and I had time to run out of the room. Nanny came after me: 'You mustn't harden your heart against your mother, my child,' she said. 'It's a mortal sin. . . .' But I ran away shouting: 'She is *not* my mother, I hate her.'

On a miserable little smallholding less than a mile from our village there lived an impoverished couple called Savelyev. Both husband and wife were old to the point of senility; their wretched house consisted of two dank and tiny rooms, and there were always tobacco shreds and ash all over the tables and chairs. Both husband and wife had long pipes clamped permanently in their mouths.

The Savelyevs had a son, but hardly anyone had ever seen him. He was sent to a military academy when still very young and had never been back to visit his parents since; all that was known about him was that he was a lieutenant-colonel serving with a regiment stationed at St. Petersburg. Suddenly, however, we heard a rumour that he had retired and would soon be returning to his parents' home.

One day when she returned home from the fields Mother was told by Nanny that young Savelyev had called; as the meal was ready she had shown him straight into the dining-room. He turned out to be about thirty-five, tall and dark and quite well dressed, and good-looking, but for the restless darting about of his gaze and a red network of veins over his cheeks and forehead. He never looked straight at the person he was talking to but kept lowering his lids and darting glances this way and that. When Mother asked what he proposed to do now he had returned to the country, he did not answer at first but shifted in an embarrassed manner in his chair; after an uneasy silence he said he was going to stay as long as possible and concern himself with his little estate. He added that he was passionately fond of shooting and expected to be going out with his gun a good deal.

When he had recovered his composure he began to ask Mother questions about her estate; she told him sadly how much time she had to spend on it, with the result that her children's education tended to be neglected. When she said that she had to wake me up in the middle of the night to give me lessons in French, Savelyev suddenly began talking to her in French; and when they reverted to Russian I found that he had offered to take over my French lessons. Mother thanked him profusely and, being a businesslike person, immediately asked him his terms; he replied that perhaps he could come for an hour and a half before dinner and, if she had no objection, would stay and have a meal with us. The old people, he said, ate nothing better than slops and he had a delicate digestion that called for properly prepared food.

Delighted with his straightforward approach, Mother said that this form of remuneration would suit her perfectly. It was not until we were having coffee that it occurred to her to ask why he had left his regiment in St. Petersburg. At the question he jumped up and, quite regardless of the fact that we were staring at him in amazement, began to pace rapidly up and down the room. After a few moments' silence he said abruptly, without looking at anyone: 'Why should anybody be interested in that? I've had enough of all this plotting and gossiping.'

He went on muttering unintelligibly and then suddenly turned, left the dining-room and disappeared from the house without even saying good-bye.

'I know it's not my place to discuss the gentry,' said Nanny, 'but I tell you this, and you can say what you like: it's a bad business if a man can't look another in the eye. You remember my words, it's a bad business.'

'What a thing to say!' cried Mother. 'Didn't you like him?'

Nanny's Last Illness

Turning suddenly to Nyuta she went on: 'He's a good-looking man.'

'Good-looking? That man?' asked my sister in horror. 'I can't even bear to look at him. His eyes keep darting about so, it's quite repulsive.'

'Just like a wolf,' agreed Nanny. 'It wouldn't matter if he were uglier, so long as he looked a bit more human.'

The next day Mother got home before my lesson began so that she could personally present the pupil to her new teacher. 'I'm so glad you are taking over from me,' she told him. 'I'm an impatient person, I'm afraid, and my poor daughter has had to endure a good deal at my hands.'

At her words Savelyev once more jumped up from his chair and began to pace up and down, saying agitatedly: 'I am impatient, too, but only with people who try to pin me down all the time. What they have against me, what they expect me to do I don't know—but they're always plotting against me and spreading rumours and slanders.'

Savelyev sighed deeply before continuing more calmly: 'Here in your house, however, I feel safe from them. I have come to feel a profound respect for you and your family, and as far as the lessons are concerned I can assure you that your daughter will never suffer as the result of my impatience. When it comes to teaching I am very patient.'

'You are a strange man, though,' Mother replied. 'This is only the second time we have met, but it is the second time you have talked about rumours and plots of which I assure you I have never heard a word. In our backwater there is usually a certain amount of gossip when a new-comer is expected, but in your case not a syllable either good or bad has been uttered.'

The lessons started. Savelyev was as good as his word and was very patient. Instead of teaching me the grammar he made me read the whole lesson page by page, repeating each

87

word after him until I could say it correctly. He translated everything for me; and at the end of the lesson was obviously far more tired than I was. His brow was covered with sweat, his cheeks were flushed and his hands were trembling.

Later lessons followed this pattern: to start with he was very attentive, explained everything to me and corrected me when I went wrong: but then he began to pay less and less attention to my reading, made no comments, and continually paced the room with his eyes on the ground. However, if I stopped reading he looked up immediately and asked why I did not go on. Sometimes he turned from pacing up and down and walked out into the hall—disappearing from the house altogether and not even returning for dinner.

Though obviously increasingly attracted to my sister Nyuta, he made no attempt to talk to her or to get to know her better. After dinner he sometimes sat himself at the table where she worked, or more often paced up and down the room—seldom saying a single word.

After dinner one day Savelyev asked Mother if he could have a word with her in private. They went into the next room together and Nanny and I went over to the Voinovs', not returning until after supper. Tired out after playing with Mitya and Olga, I went straight to bed: Nanny settled down at the table to knit a sock.

Suddenly Nyuta ran into the room and threw herself at Nanny's feet. 'Help me, Nanny darling,' she cried through her sobs, burying her head in Nanny's lap. 'You're the only one who can rescue me!'

'Don't be silly, get up at once,' grumbled Nanny, lifting her up and sitting her on a chair beside her. 'Whatever's happened? My dear child, what *is* the matter with you?'

Choking through her tears, Nyuta said that Savelyev had asked if she would be his wife—and that Mother had given no definite answer. She had not refused her permission but merely said that she would think it over and he would have to wait: which meant that she would be making her mind up one way or the other without taking Nyuta's wishes into consideration.

Nanny was staggered by the news. 'Oh, my poor darling. . . . God help us, what a terrible thing for you. Of course, I'll do my best to persuade Mother against it, but I'm afraid there's little chance of success. She's so pleased with the result of his teaching Liza that he's quite won her over.'

'But surely Mother won't ruin my life just because of my sister's lessons? I can't marry him, I can't. I can't bear to look at him even.'

'I'll tell you what to do,' said Nanny. 'You're a good girl, my dear, the sort who always listens to her mother and doesn't contradict—you try to be brave and go and see her tomorrow morning—don't reproach her, don't argue, just get on your knees and beg her not to make you marry someone you don't love. Beg her to give him a definite refusal, so that he gets the idea out of his silly head that he can carry off a pretty girl like you from the best family in the place.'

The next morning Nyuta went to Mother as Nanny had advised, but in her hurry to get to work Mother hardly listened. To her pleas that Savelyev's proposal be rejected she said merely that she herself was not eager to accept but that it needed thinking about carefully just the same. In any case, she said, there was no point in giving him an immediate refusal because it would only make him give up his lessons.

Things calmed down after this and Nyuta had high hopes that she would not be forced to enter this detestable marriage after all.

One night Nanny, who had been coughing badly for some time, had such a bad attack that Mother and Nyuta came running into our room. They tried various remedies, such as melting sugar in a spoon over a candle and giving Nanny the syrup to suck; giving her hot milk to drink; rubbing her chest with candle-grease; and covering her with warm blankets. But none was any use and it was morning before Nanny could settle down.

After this she was continually racked by coughing. She began to be feverish and to perspire; she grew thinner and thinner and soon was unable to leave her bed. Mother was so worried that she sent horses to town for the doctor and begged him in a letter to come; the whole household was sworn to secrecy. The story given to Nanny was that the doctor was visiting a neighbour and had come over to examine her as well.

At the time I was not told what he said about her, and it was not until much later I heard he had diagnosed tuberculosis: though even then I did not realize how serious this was. A subsequent conversation between Mother and my sister completely reassured me.

'Surely tubercular people spit blood,' Nyuta was saying. 'Nanny never has. I'm sure the doctor must have made a mistake. She was terribly thin last spring, and coughed a lot, before she went to Kiev; I'm sure she'll be better again when the warm weather comes.'

Our beds, that is to say Nanny's and mine, were moved out into the big hall. Whether the doctor had advised this so that the patient could breathe more easily, or whether it was Mother's idea, I don't know: but from that time on Nanny always lay there. It never occurred to anybody that tuberculosis might be catching, and in any case Mother would never have dared to part me from Nanny.

I sat beside her each day and told her what was going on: I also repeated the conversation about her between Mother and Nyuta. She looked at me sadly, patted me with her thin hand and instead of answering me said more than once: 'I do wish I could see Sasha just once more. . . .'

When I told Mother she decided that Nanny's wish must be gratified at all costs. It was three weeks before Easter, when there were no lessons at the *pensionnat* and Sasha would be free until the spring examinations; Mother made up her mind immediately, sent for the bailiff at once to arrange for the journey, and dispatched a carriage for Sasha to Vitebsk at dawn the next day.

It was two years since any of us had seen Sasha, and when a slim young lady taller than Nyuta stepped down from the carriage we hardly recognized the thin and anxious Sasha of the last days before her departure. We crowded round her for quite a while, amazed to see her grown so tall and eager to hear about her journey and where she had stayed the night. Sasha answered our questions readily and hugged us over and over again.

Dunyasha, the maid who had accompanied her to the *pensionnat*, kissed our hands in order of seniority; and when all the greetings were over Sasha ran in to see Nanny. Eagerly she kissed the sick woman on the face, eyes and forehead; then she began kissing her hands until Nanny summoned up the strength to pull them away.

The rest of the family came into the room and settled round her bed; Nanny did not say a word and put her fingers to her lips to show she was unable to speak, but she held Sasha's hands and could not take her eyes off her face. The tears streamed down her face but after a little while she controlled herself enough to stroke my sister's face and whisper: 'Give me just one more kiss.' Before long she signed that she wanted to rest and we all left the room.

In the evening we gathered round her bed again and Mother showed her a letter: 'Look, I'll read you what

Sasha's headmistress says about her,' she said. Sasha ran towards the door but Mother told her to come back; Nanny raised herself up in bed on her pillows.

'During her time with us', Mother began, 'Sasha has proved herself the pride of the *pensionnat*, our favourite and the most outstanding pupil. In your daughter's case considerable ability has, for the first time in our experience, been matched by great diligence. She is always prepared to assist her friends and new-comers to the *pensionnat* who may have been badly prepared for their studies here, a feature of her character which has endeared her to us all. It would, however, be wrong of me to fail to draw your attention to her one great defect; in spite of her brilliant progress and the perfection she has achieved in all subjects properly studied by a young girl of noble birth, she remains dissatisfied and has shown herself obstinately determined to step beyond the educational limits proper to her station in life. With this aim she has stooped to every trick and (it pains me greatly to have to report this of our favourite) even tells lies to obtain in the town books and commentaries quite unnecessary for a young lady; she studied them at night in the duty-room, which she nearly burned down because she forgot to extinguish her candle. I am forced, Madam, to draw your attention to this passion of your daughter's for study; praiseworthy as it might be in a man, it is in a young lady of noble birth a defect which must not be allowed to hamper her chances of either a successful life or a successful marriage.'

The letter concluded: 'For my part, I beg you to remember that there will always be a place for your daughter in my *pensionnat*. I should be delighted to offer her a position as a teacher, and despite her youth and inexperience am prepared to train her as my closest associate; though I would never forgive myself if I did not make it quite clear to you that the salary of a teacher at a *pensionnat* is much more modest than what she could command as a governess in the household of a well-to-do landowner.'

Tears of joy rolled down Nanny's face as she lay propped up on her pillows to listen, and as soon as she could speak she asked Mother to leave the letter under her pillow so that Sasha could read it over to her again: 'Though of course there's no need for Sasha to go anywhere as a governess,' she commented.

'I'm not scared of being a governess,' Sasha said gaily. 'I tried it last summer, and really it's not a bad job at all.'

'Of course, Sasha would know how to behave whoever's household she was in,' observed Mother.

'Oh, no,' Nanny persisted, 'there really isn't any need for her to work as a governess. You can't always be sure of finding a good place, and in any case she's too young—she deserves to get some enjoyment out of life.'

'I get plenty of enjoyment as it is,' my sister replied. 'When I sealed up my salary in an envelope for Mother I positively trembled with happiness. And just think what fun it would be to buy you an angora shawl and really soft, warm boots, Nanny!'

'What an angel you are, always thinking of others! But tell me truly, isn't there anything you want for yourself?'

'Of course there is, something I want terribly badly. I suppose I shouldn't even think about it, but I want what the Principal reproaches me with in her letter.'

'Mercy on us, but you've already learned everything there is to know!'

'I know the alphabet, and that's all. If only I could really study, the way men do. That's what I want!'

For a whole week Nanny seemed to be feeling better, and we had a wonderful time. Sasha told us about various things that had happened to her at the *pensionnat* and about the summer she had spent as a governess in the province of

Chernigov; we all felt that the black cloud under which we had been living had rolled away. One morning, however, I was roused by Nanny crying out loudly; I rushed over to her and found that she was lying down with her eyes closed but talking, talking incessantly. I called out to her and touched her hand but she went on muttering deliriously, so I ran barefoot and in my nightshirt to Mother. She came hurrying in with my sisters and although they put vinegar-soaked rags on her forehead she remained delirious all day. By evening she was a little calmer, though obviously in a very serious condition: she summoned the strength that remained to her and asked Mother to stay with her alone. Feeling lost and frightened the rest of us came out into the dining-room. How much longer Mother remained with Nanny I cannot remember, but suddenly the door was flung noisily open.

Mother ran in, hugged me to her, and cried: 'This is a terrible day for you, my darling—a tragedy, my child.' From her incoherent exclamations I gathered the one fact that Nanny was dying, or by now might be dead. With it came a completely adult realization that this was a far greater tragedy for me than the death of my own mother would have been: in effect I had already been left an orphan, and from now on all kinds of horrors and misfortunes would be coming my way. I felt as though an enormous icy lump in my heart was growing larger and larger; the blood froze in my veins and the tears on my face, and my legs and arms were cold as ice.

Nanny remained conscious until she died. She bade us all farewell, saying that she would have liked to live long enough to see me grown up but that the Lord had decided otherwise. She spoke very quietly and slowly, with lengthy pauses and a good deal of repetition. Her death came that night.

Mme Voinov took Sasha and me straight to her place from

the cemetery. I was put to bed and covered with a warm blanket; Mme Voinov and Olga Petrovna stayed with me, putting bottles at my feet, giving me mustard poultices and making me drink lime-flower tea. Sasha bent over me clutching at her heart as though afraid it would burst and repeating tenderly: 'Do cry, darling, do try to cry, it'll make you feel better.'

Mother came to fetch us the next day. The thought of the terrible things that awaited me at home—finding Nanny's bed empty and knowing I should never see her again—suddenly came over me more strongly than ever; I began tossing about on the bed and it was as though the ice in me was melting. I sobbed and screamed like a wounded animal, and it did make me feel better. Then I looked straight at Mother and shouted bitterly: 'I *won't* go home. I *hate* our house without Nanny.'

Unaccustomed to such impertinence from her daughters, Mother recoiled: but evidently decided, after a few moments' immobility, that my words were prompted only by illness and despair, so she overcame her annoyance and tried to calm me down. She couldn't allow me to cause such trouble in other people's houses, she said—but Mme Voinov asked her not to take us away and Sasha and I remained where we were.

Although it was not yet spring the days were very mild and after dinner we all sat out on the veranda. I was wrapped up well and placed in an arm-chair, and the Voinovs sat round a table near by. Sasha told us about her life at the *pensionnat* and recounted stories she had read; grown-ups as well as children listened, and Mme Voinov told her several times: 'Your mother may think we find it a nuisance having you here, but life is so much more interesting when you are! I do wish you could spend the summer with us, Sasha: it would be such a pleasure for me, and so good for the children.'

A Russian Childhood

Mother and Nyuta came over a day or two later as we were sitting down to dinner. This time we heard some of the decisions which were to have such a far-reaching effect on our lives: Mother had resolved to send Sasha back to Vitebsk in a few days' time so that she could come back sooner after the examinations—although they had said at the *pensionnat* that she could take them at any time. She had also written to her brothers in St. Petersburg asking them to get me a place at one of the Government institutes there. Sasha was to finish at the *pensionnat* at the earliest possible moment so that she could prepare me for entrance to the institute—and also be present at Nyuta's wedding.

At this startling piece of news everybody turned instinctively to Nyuta, but she sat overwhelmed and speechless. Mother told Mme Voinov: 'You always say how wonderful my children are, but however much I explain they just do not appreciate my position. They seem to think they're royal princesses. . . .'

'No, really,' Mme Voinov broke in, 'you truly have no cause for complaint. Your daughters are model girls. Sasha is already completing her education without putting you to the slightest inconvenience or expense—she's mastered several languages and can speak them like a native. Nyuta is managing the household wonderfully; she's a hard worker and never disobeys you in anything.'

'Hard worker? Never disobedient?' cried Mother. 'Children must not and dare not be disobedient to their parents. If one of my daughters forgot the fact for one second I should be very quick to remind her of it!'

Then, calming down a little, she went on more reasonably: 'I've always made it quite clear to them, and in any case they can see with their own eyes, that they are quite penniless: but at the very moment when they should be taking the fact into consideration it conveniently flies out of their heads.'

She nodded at Nyuta and continued: 'This one is told that Savelyev has proposed to her, but what do you think? She comes out with all kinds of silly remarks such as "I'm too scared. . . . His eyes are wild. . . . He frightens me. . . . I'm too young. . . . He's too old for me"; and when I told her the other day that her marriage was a family necessity she even tried to scare me by saying that she'd throw herself in the lake because she hated him so much. You see what they do, Mme Voinov, just when they could be showing their mother their obedience and trust? Naturally I don't pay any attention to such nonsense.'

Then Mother turned to my sister. 'Nyuta, why do you think that the law demands that children must obey their parents implicitly? Do you imagine it was enacted just for fun? No, the law exists because parents can tell from experience what is best for their children far better than the children themselves.'

Throughout the whole of the meal, Mother was the only one who spoke. Having staggered everyone with her announcement, she went on to tell us her plans in detail.

She had worked everything out down to the smallest point. I had to be prepared for my entrance examinations not merely well but brilliantly, so as to get a high placing at once and finish my studies with a gold medal. Medals, said Mother, were vital for a penniless girl; they ensured her a good job. The attention of the governors and staff of the institute should be attracted from the very outset, so Savelyev—who had shown what he could do in teaching me French—was to prepare me for the examinations. 'That means he'll have to join the household,' Mother continued. 'I know he would want to make himself useful to the family whose bread he and his wife will be eating.'

At this point Mother informed us how delighted Savelyev had been when she had hinted that he and Nyuta might live with us. 'Of course the idea of the marriage does not enthral me,' she added. 'He's as poor as a church mouse. All his property amounts to is a wretched little two-roomed house, and they cannot possibly live there. But what else can I do? It's no use dreaming of a son-in-law with vast estates. . . . I admit his odd behaviour worries me a little, but when they live with us I'll knock all the nonsense out of his head.'

She turned to Nyuta. 'You silly little thing, why are you taking such a wretched view of the marriage? Do you imagine your own Mother would do anything to make you unhappy? We'll make all the arrangements for you. You and your husband will be completely left to yourselves for a while, and Sasha can take Liza's lessons. Later on, of course, you'll both have to get down to some hard work.'

No one disputed Mother's observations about marriage and parental authority. In those days it was customary for marriages to be arranged; but Mme Voinov, who knew from personal experience what it was like to be married to someone she did not love, must have been terribly sorry for my sister. I saw her in tears after dinner, when Mother had gone to have a rest; Nyuta was crying on her shoulder, and Mme Voinov was making the sign of the cross over her and kissing her.

5

A Madman in the Family

Sasha managed to persuade Mother to leave me at the Voinovs until she returned from the *pensionnat*. I spent a whole month there, during which time Mother never came to see me once: a fact which surprised Mme Voinov very much. Eventually Sasha came to collect me, having come back from the *pensionnat* the day before.

It was the first time I had seen her in adult dress. She wore a beautiful long dress made in the height of fashion and a pretty summer hat and gloves, and carried a parasol. Although we knew that a new dress had been prepared for her at the *pensionnat* for the day she left, it was so strange to see any of us so smartly turned out that when I caught sight of her I stayed stock-still a few paces away.

'Sasha, my beautiful Sasha,' I thought as I looked at her; and then I ran to meet her with a sudden cry of joy. We went home by boat: as it touched the shore Dunyasha, the maid who had gone to the *pensionnat* with Sasha, met us with the news that our eldest brother Andrei had turned up on leave while Sasha had been fetching me.

'He looks a true officer,' Dunyasha reported: 'so handsome that the young ladies will never be able to leave him alone. Madam simply can't take her eyes off him. She loves him better than the rest of her children, and that's a fact.'

When Sasha heard of his arrival she ran into the house, but I lingered behind to hear the rest of the news. Mother, it seemed, had just gone over to Bukhonovo with Savelyev. 'I expect Madam wants to get him used to the business side of things,' commented Dunyasha. 'Anyhow, he can't just go on sitting about doing nothing: perhaps that's what's made him so peculiar. . . . Well, Madam will soon take him in hand.'

'Is Nyuta still crying?'

'Lord, yes, like a river. . . .'

'And where's Domna?' I asked, my heart missing a beat with apprehension.

'Madam sent her away to the farm the very minute she got back from the funeral. She didn't say why, she just told her: "Don't let me see you here again",' Dunyasha went on hurriedly. 'I shall be your only maid from now on, I'll do my very best to give satisfaction, really I will.'

When I entered the hall where my brother was chatting to my sisters he kissed me, put me on his lap, took a look at me and suddenly burst out laughing. 'Why, Liza,' he said. 'You *are* dressed in the latest Paris fashion!' Then he asked with a sad shake of his head: 'Why is she dressed like this? To think she wore this on a visit to a well-to-do household. . . . And you, Nyuta, you're not dressed any better and you're about to be married. In a decent house in St. Petersburg you wouldn't even be allowed to serve at table.'

My sisters told him that, despite our very modest standard of living, things still had to be bought for the household—though most of the money went towards the construction and repair of various farm buildings. Pig-styes and sheep-sheds had had to be rebuilt this year.

This made Andrei furious. 'What?' he shouted. 'She puts her wretched pigs and sheep before her own children?'

My sisters tried to explain that without the animals the

whole estate would go to rack and ruin and there would be nothing to eat at all.

'But that's sheer nonsense, don't you understand?' he cried. 'You're so busy thinking about the future that you let the present look after itself. As far as I'm concerned, I shall soon be absolutely independent of her. I shall be getting my pay and it'll be getting bigger; but I will *not* allow my sisters to be dressed like beggars. I'll buy you dresses myself and send them to you—if I send money she'll only spend it on improving the estate.'

Andrei went on pouring out everything that had been bottled up inside him and went on to attack the idea of Nyuta's forthcoming marriage. 'It wouldn't be so bad', he said, 'if Mother were marrying her daughter to a wealthy man in order to improve her affairs—everybody does that and it's natural enough: but to marry a girl off against her wishes merely to provide herself with a teacher and a bailiff by way of a son-in-law, really, what an idea. You mark my words, she'll come a cropper there. She thinks a stranger can be ordered about like a serf or a child, but he'll show her she's mistaken.'

Sasha interrupted her brother at this point and begged him to do something for her. 'Good heavens,' he said, 'of course I will. You must think I have no more feeling than a doorpost. . . . Tell me, what do you want me to do?'

She told him that as Mother loved him more than any of us he was the only one who could save Nyuta from this terrible marriage. She begged him to have a talk with her—and to be very careful when he did: it was no use annoying her with criticism of her decisions, all he need do was suggest that she might be quite wrong in her estimation of Savelyev.

We were all so delighted by his attitude that we ran to kiss him. He was quite touched: 'You silly little fools,' he said.

'Did you really imagine I would let anyone hurt you?'

As soon as Mother came back Andrei followed her to her room—but, being naturally hot-headed and quick-tempered, he completely forgot Sasha's warning. Abandoning any attempt at tact or diplomacy, he reproached Mother for making such marriage-plans for Nyuta. It was not long before we heard her loud and indignant tones, and then she opened the door with a bang and with one imperious thrust threw Andrei out.

He ran into our room in a fury and hurled himself on to a chair. 'Anyone would think I was still a child,' he cried, trembling with anger. 'Why, she very nearly hit me!'

Sasha put her hand over his mouth and Nyuta helped her drag him out into the garden. I ran after them.

'I was given twenty-eight days' leave but I'm not staying here a single day more,' he announced. 'I really can't stand it, it's too much.'

'I'm sure Mother would have listened to you if only you'd spoken in the way she's used to,' broke in Sasha. 'She's very fond of you, you know.'

'In that case she has a very strange way of showing it,' Andrei grumbled. 'She gazes at me in admiration, she cries, she keeps on saying I'm just like my father was, but the moment I suggest she's marrying off her daughter to the first man that comes along, just as though she were an orphan or a step-daughter, she just goes stark staring mad.'

'What have you done, what have you done?' my sisters asked in horrified tones.

'I haven't done anything, it's all your fault really. . . . If there's anything to you at all, Nyuta, you'll declare at the altar that you're being forced into the marriage by your mother.'

'Andrei, you're crazy. You know I couldn't disgrace Mother like that!'

A Madman in the Family

But at that moment we heard a carriage-bell and a smart-looking troika drew up at our steps. A well-dressed middle-aged man was helped out by a manservant; Mother was already standing at the door, and we all went out. It turned out to be Lunkovsky, one of the richest landowners in the district, whose daughter was a pupil at Sasha's *pensionnat*, though in a junior form. Lunkovsky had a rather unpleasant reputation but he had visited our house when Father was alive, and Mother received him hospitably.

Lunkovsky explained that he had been visiting a neighbour on business and taken advantage of the opportunity to call on Mother, whom he had not seen since Father's death. Now he wished to renew the acquaintance and was inviting the whole family to his place for a name-day party; but Andrei, he announced, would be coming back with him straight away. He and Andrei went off to rooms that had been prepared for them and Mother told my sisters that if they wanted to dance they could go with Lunkovsky and Andrei the next day: it would be quite easy, because Sasha had some pretty frocks and one of them could be altered for Nyuta. She herself did not intend to go. However, both of them turned down this tempting offer; Sasha said that she did not like Lunkovsky, and that neither he nor his family had a good reputation. The result was that when Lunkovsky went the next day only Andrei accompanied him.

Mother had decided to relieve Savelyev of my lessons until after the wedding, as she wanted both to give Nyuta a chance to get to know him better and also to acquaint him with the affairs of the estate by taking him out with her to see what was going on.

Sasha had to take over my lessons: how pleasantly the hours with her passed by! She arranged things so that all my written work was done in the morning, and on fine afternoons we went into the garden, where she made me read or talked to me about all sorts of fascinating things. She played games with me and ran races, and it was wonderful to be treated as a friend. I studied very hard with her and would not leave her for a minute even when our lessons were over; we grew more intimate each day and our friendship grew stronger and stronger.

Although by now his leave was coming to an end Andrei had still not returned from his visit. Mother was so worried that she sent a man over to Lunkovsky with a note, and he returned with a reply to the effect that Andrei had only stayed there for three days before going off to see someone else. He eventually turned up only the morning before the wedding and, busy as we all were with the preparations, we noticed how oddly he was behaving. He seemed absentminded and muddled and hardly spared us a glance.

Mother attributed her son's behaviour to the fact that he had spent all his leave away from home and did not bother him with any more questions. In any case she was too busy that day; there were so many orders to be given, so many notes to be written, so many people to be sent hither and thither on various errands.

The next day was the day of the wedding and there was no time to worry about Andrei; and as soon as the ceremony was over he left for St. Petersburg.

After the wedding Mother resumed her supervision of work in the fields from first thing in the morning or else went over to her brother's estate at Bukhonovo. Sasha and I continued our lessons and walks. None of us entered the rooms of the young couple, the doors of which Savelyev had had fitted with bolts. If it was fine they spent the whole day in the forest or if it rained they sat in their rooms. If we wanted Nyuta for anything we had to knock on their door—a new experience for us, who had previously had the run of the house. Nyuta, quiet by nature, now became completely silent and listless; her cheeks grew pale and her lovely blue eyes dull and lifeless. However, we saw no more of her tears and she never complained about her husband—in fact she never referred to him at all, as if she were afraid even to mention his name.

Savelyev was always uncommunicative at dinner, only answering questions addressed to him—and then briefly and very frequently off the point: it was as though he had eyes and ears for no one in the house but his wife. He ate hurriedly and greedily everything that was put in front of him, and in between the courses he turned to his wife and ran his shifty gaze restlessly over her face. Nyuta said nothing but only bent her head lower over her plate; then he would frown crossly and start drumming his fingers on the table. This always made everyone feel uncomfortable and Mother would call for the rest of the meal to be served quickly. The moment he had swallowed his last mouthful Savelyev used to rise from the table and go into his own room; if my sister ever lingered behind with us for a minute or two he would come back to the dining-room and interrupt her. 'Gossiping again?' he would ask. 'Go to your own room!' And at the sound of his voice Nyuta would give a start, jump up from her place and follow him at once.

Nyuta was in fact a rare visitor. When she sat in her room with her husband she did most of the family sewing, as before, but no longer ran the household as once she had. We all realized that this was not her fault, but Dunyasha coped very badly with the unfamiliar burden that fell upon her as a result. Mother kept Nyuta back after dinner one evening with the intention of discussing the problem, but in less than a quarter of an hour Savelyev came to the door and shouted angrily to his wife: 'That's enough of your gossiping, you can go to your room at once.'

Mother flushed all over her face, lost control of herself,

and shouted at Savelyev all the things that until then she had kept carefully bottled up.

'How much longer do you intend to remain idle?' she cried. 'When are you going to start teaching my daughter again? When are you going to stop keeping your wife locked up and let her carry on running the house?'

Savelyev did not reply but paced up and down the room for an appreciable time; suddenly he stopped in front of Mother. His face was contorted with spasms and for some moments he was unable to utter a word. Eventually he said in a choking whisper: 'I have no wish to be either a manager for you or a bailiff or a teacher, and I refuse to allow you to make my wife into your housekeeper or dressmaker.'

Mother was beside herself. 'In that case I shall throw you out of my house!' she shouted.

'Very well,' he said, 'I shall go: but of course I shall take my wife with me.' Then he came quickly to the table, poured himself out a glass of water with shaking hands, sat down on the sofa, turned to Mother and suddenly shouted at the top of his voice: 'You miser, you skinflint—you've sucked your children dry of blood and now you want to start on me! But I shan't let you!'

With this he threw himself back on the sofa and laughed —but what a laugh . . . it echoed wildly round the house and must have been heard in the yard and in the garden.

I ran out of the room screaming, Mother and Sasha after me. We all three dashed into the nursery and, totally at a loss for words, could only huddle together as peals of terrible laughter continued to reach us.

Sasha suddenly recovered: 'Poor Nyuta, she is alone with him!' she cried, and tore herself from her mother's arms in order to run back to her sister. The laughter stopped at last. We heard a scuffling noise through the open door of our room, but stayed where we were in silence until Sasha came back. She told us that Savelyev had had a severe fit, after which he had been too weak to get off the sofa; but he was calmer now, and Dunyasha and Nyuta had taken him to his bedroom.

We did not see Nyuta until the evening of the following day. 'So you've come to see us at last!' said Mother. 'Why are you keeping away from us, why don't you come and sit with us here sometimes?'

My sister's eyes were dry, but she looked absolutely worn out and could hardly drag out her words.

'He's only just fallen asleep, that's how I was able to come. When else can I? He's often awake at night even, and he follows me wherever I go.' Nyuta leant on Mother's shoulder and took her hand. 'If you throw him out he'll take me with him; he bullies me as it is; think how much worse it might be. . . . Don't let him finish me completely!' She covered her face with her hands but did not cry, perhaps because she had no tears left.

'Nyuta, my darling Nyuta,' Mother sobbed despairingly, holding my sister to her bosom. 'I only wanted to throw him out so that you would be rid of him!'

'It is too late,' Nyuta replied miserably. 'He would find me even under the earth.'

A second catastrophe followed: a thick packet arrived in the post for Mother. Several pages from Andrei were inside and another sealed letter was enclosed. After the first page Mother clutched her forehead with horror and for a long time she could not bring herself to answer Sasha's questions. Several times she started to read the letter aloud but tears choked her and she had to give up.

In his letter Andrei begged Mother to forgive him for having spent so little of his leave at home. He told her that when he went to Lunkovsky's party he had gambled with him the next day and lost six hundred roubles; it was his despair and fear of upsetting Mother that had made him stay away. He begged her on his knees to pay this debt of honour for him—for otherwise Lunkovsky would inform his commanding officer and that would be the end of his Service career, his only hope of being able to help the family. Andrei concluded by saying that Lunkovsky had offered an easy alternative to repayment and wished to give Mother the conditions in a personal letter.

Lunkovsky's letter was very largely devoted to praise of Andrei, and his loss at cards was passed off as 'bad luck' with which Mother need not be embarrassed; the writer did, however, mention that his governess was leaving and that his music teacher, who had been engaged only for the summer, was due to go at the end of August.

'We would like', wrote Lunkovsky, 'to engage someone who could undertake both these duties, and we would be delighted if Mlle Sasha would agree to teach my daughters. Another point is that my wife, whose eyesight has been poor these last few years, has been needing a reader for a long time now; perhaps your daughter could undertake this duty too. For all these services I would pay her 100 roubles a month; I have been paying 50 for language lessons and 30 for music, and my wife would make up the other 20 for having her letters written at her dictation and for being read to. It would make us extremely happy if you and your daughter could accept our proposition.'

Mother read the letters over and over again, crying and cursing both Andrei and Lunkovsky.

'Never mind,' said Sasha, trying to calm her. 'I can take up my job at the *pensionnat* in September, as they suggested, and——'

'What's the point of that now?' Mother broke in. 'They are more generous with praise than salaries. A miserable thirty-five roubles a month is the most they will offer you, and you might make another fifteen from private lessons; we could never pay off the debt that way. No, you'll have to take the job with Lunkovsky whether you want to or not.'

After a long silence Sasha said in an unsteady voice that according to what she had heard in the *pensionnat* and from Lunkovsky's daughter, governesses seldom stayed there long, and she had even been told in as many words by the head-mistress that governesses had poor treatment in his household. Mother cried and hugged Sasha as she listened but ended up by talking about the job with Lunkovsky as if it were all settled. 'You'll be able to stand on your own feet wherever you are,' she said cheerfully.

In conversation with Mother the next day Sasha begged her to arrange for the priest to give me lessons; and also implored Dunyasha, who had grown fond of her while they were at the *pensionnat*, to teach me to sew and to crochet and to see I was never left alone. Sasha made Mother promise not to wake me up at night for lessons but to take me for French, if only twice a week.

On the day of Sasha's departure we talked as animatedly at the table as if we were hurrying to say everything we could to each other. Sasha gave me some more advice and discussed various domestic arrangements with Mother. After dinner the newlyweds rose as usual to go to their own rooms but Sasha plucked up her courage and asked Savelyev if Nyuta could stay behind. Much to our surprise he immediately agreed and said that he would go over and visit the old folk. He left the house and Mother shortly afterwards went to have her rest.

Sitting in the dining-room with our backs to the open door, we did not hear him come back.

'The gathering of the crows,' he croaked, 'and only the dear Mamma is missing. . . .'

Sasha jumped up as if stung. Not realizing that Mother had come into the room and was standing just behind Savelyev, she confronted him with a stamp of her foot and began to shout at the top of her voice. 'How dare you abuse Mother in this house? Everybody hates you because you give my sister such a terrible time. I only have to give the word and the peasants will tie you up and throw you in the lake to drown!'

Savelyev was so taken aback, and so frightened at Sasha's outburst, that he could only mutter incoherently and stand like a schoolboy cowering in front of his teacher.

'What right have you to give orders in this house?' she stormed on. 'My mother is mistress here. How dare you forbid Nyuta to stay with her sisters? She stays right here, and you can get out, get out this minute.' She pointed imperiously to the door and Savelyev slunk towards it with jaws twitching and swaying as though drunk.

When we were left alone Mother congratulated Sasha on having stood up to the 'insolent scoundrel' as she had done. Pleased as we were that Nyuta had been rescued, if only for a short time, we never suspected what the sequel would be. Meanwhile our conversation was interrupted by the news that Sasha's carriage had arrived. She picked up her belongings, said good-bye, and left for the Lunkovskys'.

Long past midnight, when we were all sound asleep, a shot rang out, followed by a piercing inhuman cry. Wondering what on earth had happened we jumped from our beds. Mother lit a candle with trembling hands and of course when she ran out into the hall I followed.

In the dim light we found Nyuta lying unconscious on the floor and her husband trying to lift her. A few paces from them was a revolver.

'You killer, you murderer!' shouted Mother, rushing at

Savelyev with raised fists, quite beside herself; but he ran into the next room and Dunyasha helped Mother to lift up my sister and carry her to a bed in our room.

It is difficult to describe Mother's despair; she fell on her knees at Nyuta's side, sobbing and wringing her hands, saying that she and Savelyev were both murderers. She showered endearments on my sister, swearing to avenge her and make sure that her husband rotted in prison.

Meanwhile we discovered that Nyuta had not been wounded—Savelyev had evidently missed and my sister was simply in a deep faint. Mother gave Nyuta spirits to sniff and put water on her forehead, both quite in vain.

All the women sleeping in the kitchen were called in to help: they fussed around, made various suggestions, burned rags on a candle and put them under Nyuta's nose, thrust their fingers into Nyuta's mouth, tickled her under the arms —all quite ineffectively. Eventually their prolonged experiments ended in Nyuta's stirring and opening her eyes. Mother gave a shout of joy which turned out more like a groan. Kissing her face and hands, she cross-questioned her about what had happened, but despite her persistence could get no reply. Nyuta barely moved her lips and large tears rolled slowly down her pale face.

When she was undressed to be put to bed, Dunyasha pointed out bruises and weals all over her body, but although Mother again began urgently questioning her about them she remained silent. With tears streaming down her face Mother threw herself on her knees before the icons, crying desperately: 'O God, why do you punish her? She is only a child. It is the murderer who deserves to die—and strike me also, for I am guilty too!' Then she sat down by Nyuta's bed and begged her in the name of all that was holy to explain the shot and how she had come to faint and about the bruises on her body.

Dunyasha went to heat the samovar so that my sister could have a cup of hot tea, and the three of us were alone in the room. I sat quietly close to Mother's knee, afraid to miss a single word Nyuta might say. Swallowing back her tears and speaking with such an effort that it seemed every word was being dragged out of her, Nyuta gave Mother the following explanation. . . .

Her husband had realized from the very first that she could not love him, and he grew furious at every sign she gave of affection and care for the family. He was jealous of her mother and sisters and to find her in animated conversation with any of us enraged him. He forbade her to have anything to do with her younger sisters and longed to alienate her from her family. Morose and suspicious, he invariably cross-examined her on any conversation she had with her relatives and always wanted to know what she had been smiling about. If she was unhappy he thought she had been complaining about him to us, and if she was gay he imagined we had been laughing together about him. He watched every step she took, complaining the whole time and angrily accusing her of lying about everything. At first he had only cursed her but recently he had begun to beat her and ill-treat her. Driven beside himself by the scene with Mother and Sasha, he had thrown himself at her but she had managed to escape and run into the hall. He rushed after her and shot at her, but it was dark in the hall and he missed.

Although Mother kept on saying 'But he's mad!' she did not really appreciate that he actually was.

Nyuta spent the whole day in our part of the house. Savelyev turned up in the evening but Mother refused to let him in and shouted out an angry catalogue of his misdeeds at him, including the things that Nyuta had asked her not to repeat. She called him a scoundrel and a murderer, cursed him, threatened to have him locked up for shooting at Nyuta and to let him rot in prison, and said she would put in a full report to the authorities.

Savelyev made no attempt to answer, let alone justify himself; and when Mother looked him straight in the eye and advanced on him shouting curses he was really terrified and backed to the door.

After a few days he quietened down; Nyuta recovered and was calmer. Just then we heard that Savelyev's father had died, and he began to go to his parents' place daily to put his tiny property in order. How he arranged his affairs no one inquired, though we did hear that he had let the whole of it for a few roubles a year. The sale of his father's things brought him a hundred roubles or so and he took a year's rent in advance; this *coup* had a calming effect on him for a short while, and when he came and demanded his wife again there was nothing she could do but return to him.

Spring had come. Savelyev had been suffering from a cough for some time, but now it grew much worse and when he had a coughing fit it echoed all over the house as loudly as a hammer striking an anvil. His breath whistled and rattled in his throat and he gasped until it seemed as though he would choke at any moment. The spasms left him so helpless that he could only sit still, bathed in sweat and with a high colour in his cheeks. Often he spat blood.

'He must have consumption,' Mother told Nyuta. 'He won't last long, and really I can't pretend . . . the sooner the better!'

But when there was no haemorrhage Savelyev felt better and started going for long walks again, dragging his wife with him everywhere—and, just as before, refusing to let her out of his sight. Suddenly he started paying attention to me: the man who hardly ever spoke to any member of the household now began coming into my room and sitting beside me on the porch, looking at my toys and asking whether there was any news of Sasha.

One day he came back from the shop—it was in the village about two miles away—with a large parcel and announced he had brought me a present. When I told Mother about it all she was genuinely pleased. 'Tell him not to waste his money on sweets and rubbish like that,' she suggested. 'Ask him to talk to you in French instead, or read a book with you.'

Nyuta's reaction to his change of attitude was quite different. 'You must try to keep away from him,' she said. 'I'm sure there's something behind it.'

He always pestered me with questions when he came back from a walk—had anyone asked for him, or had anything interesting happened. If he had been over to his parents' house, where his wife seldom accompanied him, he always questioned me about Nyuta, whom he seemed to regard as the villain of the piece. My answer was always the same: Nyuta had been to see me for a few moments but otherwise had stayed in her room. Once I had made my customary report when Savelyev shouted: 'How dare you lie to me?' and dragged me to the window looking on to the yard, where we could see Nyuta standing in front of the barn talking to the cook and a village lad.

She had obviously been giving orders over some household matter; I said I couldn't watch every step she made and that she must have just come out. At this Savelyev clutched my shoulders in an iron grip and, his restless gaze momentarily still, stared into my eyes. Almost unable to contain his fury, he spaced out his words one by one and said that when he was away from the house I must stop playing and keep a sharp watch to see what the others were doing. I must find out every word spoken by my sister to anybody else, keep my ears open until I knew everything that was going on, and then report to him: he said that if I hid anything from him or told a lie he would thrash me until he drew blood. If I dared breathe a word of anything he had said things would be still worse for me.

Astounded by the way he had pulled me about and what he had said, I stayed motionless by the window where he had dragged me as he left the room and returned with a packet. 'Here are your sweets,' he said, throwing them on the table. 'Eat them, but remember what I've said.'

So furious that I forgot to be frightened, I snatched them up and threw them in his face. 'Curse you, damn you—you must be possessed!' I screamed.

Sweets and biscuits scattered all over the floor: Savelyev took hold of my shoulders and threw me to the ground as hard as he could. He began to hit me all over and when I screamed he stopped for a moment, holding me down with one hand and getting out his handkerchief—presumably to gag me—with the other; but at this moment the door flew open and Nyuta ran to my aid. She shouted as she tried to protect me that somebody would come in and then Mother would hear about it: he pushed her angrily to one side, kicked me several times, and left the room with Nyuta after him. Outraged by what had happened I could hardly wait for Mother to return so that I could tell her about it, and I was still upset and furious when my sister came back. Tearfully I showed her the scratches and bruises left by her husband's boots; Nyuta hugged me and her tears fell on my face and hands. Then she started cursing her mad husband and her own wretched life with him, reproaching Mother dreadfully for having married her against her will to such a cruel beast.

Such words from Nyuta, who was normally so placid, and her frankness with me made me feel close to her for the first time. When she begged me not to tell Mother I refused at first and said that she would have Savelyev tied up and thrown on the manure-cart for sticks and stones to be thrown at him until his head was broken; but Nyuta only smiled sadly and tried as hard as she could to explain that as her husband was not a serf but of noble birth, like Mother, the most she could do was to have him thrown out of the house. 'And if she does that', said Nyuta, 'he will certainly take me with him, and then I shall be completely at his mercy.'

This persuaded me at last, and I promised my sister to keep quiet no matter what should happen to me.

I now had a fresh danger to face, and had to use my cunning and agility not to be left alone with Savelyev: it involved running over to our neighbours, from them into the nearest peasants' huts or to the farm, and hiding from him in hay-lofts or barns or scrambling into bushes and ditches.

When he did catch me I never surrendered without a struggle. If he unexpectedly came across me alone in a room I jumped up as soon as he opened the door and threw books or vases or anything which came to hand at him; if he did succeed in catching me I spat at him and bit his hands and shouted until he got a gag in my mouth. Then he would tie me on to a table and thrash me with the leather strap which he now always carried in his pocket until he drew blood— but as soon as he heard a door slam or a cart rattling across the yard he took fright and ran out of the room. Usually Nyuta came to my rescue.

One day his own serf brought Savelyev word that his mother was dying, and he went to her at once. There was no one left in the house but Nyuta and myself, and I noticed that she seemed very preoccupied: she was bustling about the place and running busily between the farm and the village. Various women came to see her and there was a good deal of whispering.

All this fascinated me, and to find out what was going on I went into the maid's room and discovered Dunyasha with a black cockerel in her arms: and a strange old woman was sitting there with a black cat and a bundle of some kind. Running to Nyuta to ask what was happening, I found her hurriedly looking through a chest of drawers and pulling out various articles of clothing belonging to her husband. Telling me that I must not tell Mother anything of what I might see and hear, she explained: 'Everyone says that Savelyev is possessed, so I called in the wise-woman to see whether she could take the curse off him.'

She picked up her husband's things and we went to the room where the wise-woman was. Giving me the cockerel to hold, Dunyasha ran into the kitchen and returned with a pan of charcoal: she put the pan on the fire and, muttering some kind of chant, sprinkled the charcoal with powders and dried herbs. Then she picked up Savelyev's clothes and held them over the smoke which was rising from the pan: next she took the cockerel, held it with its tail towards the pan, cut the tip of a tail-feather off and threw it on the charcoal—after which the cockerel was thrown tail-first out of the window. The cat she treated slightly differently: the tip of its tail was scorched on the charcoal and despite its mewing and scratching and struggling she held to it tightly until she had cut off the scorched patch of fur. This she gave my sister with the instructions, 'Sprinkle it on his food a bit at a time'. And then the cat, too, was thrown tail-first out of the window to the accompaniment of continued muttering.

Watching with unblinking eyes every movement the wise-woman made, I did not notice the door open and Savelyev's tousled head come round it. 'Get out of here, get out,' he shouted, pulling me by the hand.

'But you're all right now,' I cried tearfully: 'the wise-woman took the curse off you!' But he dragged me along to the nursery, locked the door to keep Nyuta out, and thrashed me once again.

The bloody weals on my body took a long time to heal, and I suffered considerable pain. To hide the evidence of her husband's brutality Nyuta told Mother that she would take me to the bath-house because Dunyasha could not manage my thick hair; indifferent as ever to what her children did, Mother raised no objection.

Early one morning Nyuta ran into our room saying that her husband was very ill and asking if the doctor could be sent for. We had heard a few days previously that a land-owner living some eight miles away had a relative who was an army doctor from St. Petersburg staying with him, and Mother sent horses over for him at once.

When he entered the sickroom there were exclamations of surprise from both him and his patient, and it turned out that they had served in the same regiment. After examining the sick man and talking to him for a while the doctor came into the dining-room to see Mother and Nyuta: I ran in from the nursery, where I had been praying God on my knees that the doctor would pronounce Savelyev fatally ill.

Actually what the doctor said surpassed all our expectations. First of all he said how surprised he was that Savelyev had lived with us so long without our realizing that he was mentally unbalanced: according to him, Savelyev's condition had been discovered a few years before his dismissal from the service. His attacks had usually taken the form of mercilessly thrashing his batman for no reason. His fellow officers had disliked him and often told him to his face that he was mad. When his condition worsened and his behaviour became completely intolerable he was dismissed; but as there was no question of his serving elsewhere the authorities took no steps to inform anyone of his condition. Since then his state had, in the doctor's opinion, greatly deteriorated: in their ten-minutes' conversation he had told the doctor that he was surrounded by enemies plotting his destruction; he was suffering from a persecution complex. The doctor added that he was in the last stages of consumption and unlikely to live more than another week or two.

Much to our surprise Nyuta burst into tears when she heard all this. Sobbing and lamenting, she begged the doctor not to tell anyone about her husband's madness: she had had to suffer so much during his lifetime that she did not want to be branded with the shame of having been the wife of a lunatic.

Soon the doctor's prognosis proved correct and Savelyev died. When the time came for the funeral Mother took me over to stay with the Voinovs. Playing with the children and enjoying the calmer atmosphere of their house had a beneficial effect and I grew stronger and more relaxed, and felt happier.

When I got home I heard that Mother had had a letter from my uncle suggesting that she should bring me to St. Petersburg in August. A very influential general, he had managed to get me a place in the Smolny Institute. He enclosed in his letter the curriculum for which I had to be prepared.

At first I was delighted with the news that I should be leaving my home for good before long, but then the thought of having to wait until autumn began to depress me, for I was firmly convinced that under my parents' roof I could experience nothing but misfortune.

Mother wrote to Sasha telling her to terminate her teaching as soon as she could in order to come home and start preparing me at once for the various subjects in the Institute's curriculum; with Sasha's salary and the money saved from the household expenses, she added, there was enough to pay for all of us to go to St. Petersburg.

Soon Sasha returned, and I happily started preparing for the entrance examinations: in spite of intensified lessons every day I felt stronger and better. The future held no fears for me, and the day when I should leave my parents' home was approaching fast.

6

Starting at Smolny

One clear cold October morning I arrived with my mother at the Smolny Institute for the Daughters of Noblemen.

The high walls, like a nunnery's, which from now on were to separate me from my family and the easy-going ways of life on a country estate did not alarm me in the least—nor did the stout porter in a red uniform who threw open the gates of the Institute for us, for I was full of bright hopes and preoccupied with new impressions and my journey to St. Petersburg.

We had just taken our coats off when a woman came into the entrance-hall with a girl of about my own age. I wanted to run up to her but at this moment the mistress on duty made her appearance; she was fat and middle-aged with a sharp pasty face and narrow eyes. Barely acknowledging our greeting, she asked us all to follow her into the reception room.

Mme Golembiovsky, the other girl's mother, and my mother began to apologize for having brought their children three months later than the proper day owing to difficult domestic circumstances and the distances they had had to travel; unsatisfied by the explanations the mistress grumbled at them all the way from the entrance-hall to the reception room, her complaining tones echoing along the vast corridors like the creaking of an unoiled wheel.

A bell rang and two people came in: a monitress to examine us in French and a master in Russian. The examination was simple and we both passed; in a few minutes the duty mistress reappeared and led both us girls away with her down cold and endless corridors to see the Directress. Our mothers were sent for as well, but being 'outsiders' were not allowed to walk along the corridors of the Institute but had to go outside into the street, walk round the building and enter the apartments of the Directress through the other gate.

I was so keen to see my new friends that, in spite of the mistress's severe appearance, I turned to her as soon as we entered the corridor and asked: 'Where are the girls, Auntie?'

'I am not your aunt,' she replied brusquely. 'You must call me Mlle Tufayev.'

Silenced immediately by the snub, for the rest of the way I could only look at my companion, who was walking beside me with bent head and quivering shoulders. Our mothers were already waiting for us at the doors of the Directress's spacious reception room, which we all entered together.

Maria Pavlovna Leontyev, Directress of the Smolny Institute, sat on a couch against the opposite wall; on a chair beside her was her lady-companion Olenkina.

The Directress was an old woman with pendulous cheeks and faded expressionless eyes, and the smile fixed on her lips was more of a grimace. She looked as though she had just swallowed something bitter; her haughty appearance seemed to frighten the Golembiovsky girl.

'Mummy, Mummy,' she screamed suddenly, throwing herself into her mother's arms.

'Be kind enough to come closer,' croaked the Directress in a bad-tempered quaver. 'Here, a little nearer still. First of all I must ask you to conclude this . . . demonstration. You may be seated'—and she imperiously waved Mme Golembiovsky to a chair opposite her table; at which my companion ran to her mother and clutched her skirts.

The Directress turned back to Mme Golembiovsky. 'Do you see what spoiled and ill-mannered children you pass on to us?'

'Spoiled?' repeated Mme Golembiovsky with astonishment. 'I assure you, Madame, that my daughter is an obedient, affectionate and responsive child. How can you say such a thing when you do not know her?' But she had no chance to finish, for Olenkina rushed over and hissed in a furious whisper clearly audible all over the room: 'You must call the Directress "Your Excellency", and please remember not to address her so informally.'

'I beg your pardon, Your Excellency,' said Mme Golembiovsky in embarrassed tones. 'I'm afraid I did not address you correctly. I live in the provinces and do not appreciate the finer points; but nevertheless I must repeat that my daughter has a heart of gold. Her father's dead and she needs to be mothered'; and tears poured from the poor woman's eyes.

'Mummy, I'm frightened,' cried the girl suddenly.

'Madame, my reception room is not the place for family scenes,' said the Directress. 'Will you be good enough to take your daughter outside and wait there for the form-mistress.' Then, turning her head slightly towards my mother, the Directress indicated that she was prepared to listen to what she had to say.

Knowing that the use of French was a social advantage, Mother addressed her in that language. This was obviously the right thing to do, for the Directress graciously inclined her head—a fact which could only be deduced from the fact that her tall starched head-dress quivered slightly. Her behaviour with everybody was stiff and stilted, for her feeling of self-importance did not allow her to listen to anything more than 'Yes, Your Excellency' and 'No, Your Excellency' from anyone, let alone embark on a lengthy conversation. In consequence her interview with Mother lasted only a few minutes, during which time the Directress looked straight over our heads. I learned later that she never looked anyone straight in the eye and when she gave orders to her subordinates or listened to their reports she always directed her cold stare somewhere into the distance.

We went back as we had come: the girls with Mlle Tufayev, the mothers separately. This time the silence was broken by my companion's sobs, and when we returned to the room where we had been examined they were already sitting there —and she threw herself tearfully into her mother's arms at once.

'I must ask you to stop this howling,' Mlle Tufayev said sharply. 'When I return in a few minutes to fetch the girls we shall do it ourselves, but meanwhile it is still your responsibility.'

'Dear Mlle Tufayev,' Mme Golembiovsky begged her, 'do say just one kind word to Fanny, anything you like. Her heart must be flapping like a little bird's from all these interviews.'

'Flapping? What an extraordinary expression!' was the scornful reply. ' "*Be quiet!*", that's what you ought to tell your daughter. You upset the Directress with your unnecessary fussing and now you're starting all over again.' And she turned away to the door.

'Do as she says, my darling: stop crying, dear heart,' said Mme Golembiovsky, kissing her daughter affectionately and ignoring the fact that Mlle Tufayev had stopped and was watching them. 'What can we do' sweetheart? The people here must have hearts of stone.'

'Oh!' cried Mlle Tufayev. 'I shall inform the Directress at once of the instructions you are giving your daughter.'

'Do take pity on the poor woman,' my mother well-meaningly begged her. 'You can see how upset she is.' But she was pushed rudely out of the way, and at that moment Fanny Golembiovsky screamed and fell on the floor in a faint. Mlle Tufayev hurried out and some maids came running in and carried poor Fanny to the sickroom with her mother following.

I said good-bye to my mother quickly and went with Mlle Tufayev, who had reappeared. She took me to a drawing class, but I was so upset—by Fanny's tears and fainting, not at parting with my mother—that I scarcely noticed my surroundings. Somehow I automatically did everything I was told without even looking at my new companions. Then the bell sounded and the girls ran up and began to ply me with questions.

'Silence! Form pairs!' cried the form-mistress as she began to arrange her pupils in order of height, pair after pair, with the smaller ones in front and the taller at the back. As she did so she watched closely to make sure the procession was orderly, pulling a girl forward here and pushing another back there until eventually she led us in strict order—marching at the head of her regiment—to the dining-room.

When we got there I was surprised to see some girls were standing against the wall or already seated at a punishment table; some had no aprons, others continued to stand after we had said grace and sat down, and odder still one girl had a piece of paper pinned to her shoulder and another a stocking. I asked my neighbour in a whisper about this and it turned out that the piece of paper indicated that the girl had played with it during a lesson and the stocking was to show that it had been badly darned.

After lunch we were formed up into a crocodile again and

led to the dormitory, where we had to put on coats and knitted bonnets before going for a walk in the garden.

Our walk lasted only half an hour, during which we strolled in the Institute garden in couples talking quietly to each other. Anyone who laughed or lagged behind or moved out of formation was pounced on by the mistress. 'What is all this silly laughter?' she would ask, and then hurry without waiting for an answer to reprimand another girl who had stepped out of line.

Being a new girl I was sent after the walk to the matron in charge of the pupils' uniforms. I was issued with a clumsy brown frock—its coffee colour distinguished us juniors from the others, so that we were always known as coffee-drops— with a round low-cut neck and short sleeves, under which went tapes tying on separate sleeves of white linen. Short ugly capes covered our bare necks and white aprons pinned at the back were worn over our dresses. Cape, sleeves and apron were all made of coarse white linen replaced by finer ones on holidays. On our feet we wore the clumsy shoes issued.

I had just changed into my uniform when a monitress came into the matron's room and said she would take me to the reception room, where my sister was waiting to see me. What a wonderful surprise this was! When I saw Sasha I threw myself into her arms, and both the warmth of my kisses and my tears told her without my putting anything into words that I was far from delighted with the Institute.

'You are a silly little thing,' she scolded me gently. 'When something completely unimportant goes wrong it weighs down on you like a millstone, and when things go well you don't even notice. . . . Mother told me what happened this morning.'

She stroked my hair. 'Don't worry, things aren't so bad. There are kind people here, you know. I have only just arrived, and I did not count on seeing you today, but I

thought I'd find out from the porter what you would be
doing, and then I met the nice monitress who brought you
here. I explained that we should only be in St. Petersburg
for a week, and inquired whom I should ask for permission
to see you every day during our short visit, and what do you
think? "I'll take you to the Principal," she said. "I am her
daughter, and I'm sure she will arrange it for you." And
let me tell you that your Principal is a very charming woman,
her kind smile and her nice looks simply amazed me—and
she gave me permission at once to see you every day until we
leave.'

I had not yet met the Principal, and hope flickered in my
heart once more as I eagerly listened to everything Sasha had
to say. This Mme Saint-Hilaire, whom the girls called
Maman, was our immediate authority; both mistresses and
pupils took their various problems to her, and the Directress
was above them all like a High Court Judge to whom only
really important matters were referred for decision.

After seeing my sister I went back to the dormitory feeling
much happier, and was extremely pleased to find that I had
been placed not in Mlle Tufayev's form but in a Mlle Verkhovsky's. She seemed pleasant and kind, greeting me with a
smile and an outstretched hand; astonished at such a welcome,
I threw myself on her neck and kissed her on the mouth. The
others, who had entered the Institute three months previously,
looked on in horror; they had had time to learn the rules and
regulations. Kissing a form-mistress on the shoulder or the
hand was considered commendably respectful, but kissing
her on the mouth was an unforgivable familiarity.

'No, no, my dear—that really is rather too demonstrative,'
said Mlle Verkhovsky as she freed herself. 'We don't behave
like that here.' But there was nothing unkind about the way
she spoke, and my feeling of happiness did not desert me.

Eventually the form-mistress retired to her room, which

was adjacent to the dormitory, and I was left alone with my new friends. The girls surrounded me at once and showered me with questions and I said at once that I was glad I had been placed in Mlle Verkhovsky's form and not Mlle Tufayev's. At this I was dragged to the far end of the dormitory away from the form-mistress's door so that she could not overhear us: all speaking at once, the girls told me that sometimes Mlle Verkhovsky treated them even worse than Mlle Tufayev, but I refused to believe them. If so, I decided, it must be their own fault and there was nothing for me to be afraid of, since I planned to be so diligent and obedient that at the end of my schooling I would get the gold medal, as I had promised Sasha and my mother.

Suddenly a girl called Masha Ratmanov broke in. 'And why were you making up to her? What did you kiss her for?'

I was very embarrassed and did not know what to say, but the others defended me on the grounds that I was new and did not know my way about yet. Then they asked me to show them what I had brought from home; arms were linked and together we went over to my locker, where my box had already been put. To see better we all knelt on the floor and started to take out various items—pencils, pens, a pen-knife and other classroom equipment. Then followed sweets, which I offered round, and finally from the bottom I drew out a large cardboard box.

'Now I'll show you something really lovely,' I told the girls round me; and, taking the lid off, I showed them some birds' eggs laid carefully on some wood-shavings. 'This is a lark's egg . . . a sparrow's . . . a pigeon's . . . a crow's. . . .'

'Crow's eggs! You country bumpkin!' Masha Ratmanov roared with laughter and hit the cardboard box as hard as she could so that all my eggs, which I had treasured for so many years, fell out and broke.

Starting at Smolny

I burst into tears.

'That was a nasty, mean thing to do,' one of the girls told Masha: but, quite unabashed, and smiling as triumphantly as though she had done something heroic, she marched off to the other end of the dormitory.

Masha Ratmanov was not a bad girl by nature. She was lively, witty and gay and it took her a long time to come to terms with the discipline of the Institute. Being continuously shouted at by her teachers and subjected to daily punishment and rigid regulations hardened her but it did not suppress her natural high spirits. In her free time she threw herself whole-heartedly into games and races, but this merely irritated the mistresses; she was always being caught on the scene of her 'crime', her apron was torn off her, and she was pushed into a corner or by the blackboard and solemnly lectured by the hour. Mischievous, high-spirited, and with a sharp and ready tongue, Masha began to answer back right and left and eventually earned herself the title of 'desperado'.

Despite her mischievousness, Masha had one fine quality— the spirit of comradeship. What the mistresses considered particularly heinous offences were punished by forbidding the other girls to speak to the culprit; she was always the first to disregard the ban, and despite strict orders made a point of talking to the victim and attacking those who obeyed the ridiculous instruction. She was always the first to stand up for anyone in disgrace. She not only teased and berated sneaks and tell-tales but, when no one was looking, she pushed them about and pinched them so hard that there were bruises on their necks and arms for ages afterwards.

Masha's nickname of 'desperado' was not coined specially for her, but was the general word for those who dared to answer the masters and mistresses back. There were girls like Masha in every form, which was hardly surprising when the Institute's avowed aim was to force everyone into the same mould. Children accustomed to kindness and affection were not only harmed by the Institute but destroyed; and this is what happened to my friend Fanny Golembiovsky.

More than three months had passed since she entered the Institute, but she had still made no appearance in either the classroom or the dormitory. She had stayed in the sickroom all this time; what was wrong with her we did not know, though the doctor's diagnosis was home-sickness.

One morning after the bell, 'Maman' came into the classroom during our German lesson followed by Fanny, who had altered so much that I scarcely recognized her. Her thin fingers pulled nervously at her apron, her long neck looked like a cord connecting her head to her body, her narrow shoulders jerked convulsively, her cheeks were sunken and her big eyes seemed larger than ever as her gaze darted restlessly from side to side. When the German master asked whether she had prepared the lesson she said that she had done no lessons during her illness; but he was so delighted at her fluent reading and translation of a page he showed her that he gave her twelve plus, the highest possible mark.

'Maman' was also present during the French lesson, when once more she read and easily translated what was given her; then the master asked her to recite something from memory. She began the poem 'Prayer', in which a child asks God to grant his mother a long life. Fanny's voice shook more and more and she said the lines with such feeling that the tears caught at her throat and she stopped in mid-sentence as though choking. The French master looked inquiringly at the Principal and then asked Fanny to write a short letter in French. She picked up a piece of chalk with trembling fingers and hurriedly wrote a few lines; when the master read it out loud, it turned out to be a letter to her mother saying that she would die if she were not taken away from the Institute.

When Fanny returned to her desk the Principal bent down

to her and said kindly: 'You are beautifully prepared, child; but what can we do to stop you feeling so miserable?'

Fanny should have been less conscious than the rest of us of the harsh conditions of life in the Institute. She slept in the warm sickroom, had special meals there much better than ours, saw her mother twice a week and was surrounded by the nicest people in the Institute—the Principal, the doctor, and the nurse; but all this was not enough, and if she had to spend a single day in the classroom or the dormitory she felt ill again.

Although she was seldom the target of the form-mistresses' anger and sarcasm, their comments made her start and turn pale every time. She did not make friends easily and only answered the other girls' questions slowly and uninterestedly.

'How horrid and cold it is here,' Fanny would say looking round and shivering.

'Here? What do you mean *here*? Do you come from a different world, Princess Touch-me-not?' cried Masha Ratmanov mockingly.

'You're rude and horrid,' answered Fanny, bursting into tears.

Fanny spent all her free time writing; finding her on one occasion bent over a sheet of paper as usual, Mlle Tufayev asked: 'What's that you're doing?' and snatched the sheets she had written out of her hands.

'A letter to Mummy.'

'What nonsense, how can you write to her when you see her twice a week? If they *are* to your mother, how do you send them to her?'

'I give them to her when she comes.'

Mlle Tufayev put aside the stocking she was for ever knitting, put on her glasses, and began to read. 'What's this. . . . You have the temerity to correspond in Polish?'

'But I am Polish,' Fanny explained.

'That's a fine thing! I shall take your letters to the Directress myself and inquire whether pupils are allowed to write home in outlandish languages and have the audacity to give the letters to their parents without first submitting them to the form-mistress. I have never since I first came to Smolny seen anyone as spoiled as you; and all because you are for ever kissing your mother, I expect—and she was the one who made things difficult for everyone, including the Directress, the moment she crossed the threshold of this establishment: either that or because you are always putting on airs and sulking and going off into a faint. . . .'

But Mlle Tufayev's monologue was interrupted by Fanny's hysterical weeping. 'What a wretched little cry-baby you are,' commented Mlle Tufayev as she made majestically for the door.

We all surrounded Fanny, gave her water and moistened her forehead; but she grew so weak from sobbing that she had to be taken to the sickroom again, and over a week passed without a sign of her in class.

One morning just as we were getting up we heard running in the corridors and rushed out to see what was happening; maids, sickroom servants and form-mistresses came running past shouting to us to get back to our dormitories, and we scuttled back like mice to their holes. A monitress ran in and told Mlle Verkhovsky that the Principal wanted to see her immediately; we coffee-drops, consumed with curiosity, ran out again to investigate and, stopping a passing maid, begged her to tell us what had happened.

'Shouldn't dream of it,' she said decidedly. 'When less than this happens we're forbidden to tell you; but when it's something like *this* . . .' and she pushed us out of the way and disappeared.

This of course heightened our curiosity still further, and as usual it was our 'desperado' who decided to do something about it. Descending to the lower floor, where we coffee-drops were not allowed to go alone, Masha Ratmanov risked being caught at every step but solved the mystery by giving a five-kopeck bribe to one of the stokers. It turned out that Fanny Golembiovsky had tried to run away.

Early that morning, wearing a coat and with a scarf over her head—she must have hoped to be mistaken for a maid on an errand to the shops—she had run out of the sickroom and into the street; but the porter realized what was happening and caught her not far from the gates of the Institute.

We had barely recovered from this staggering piece of information when a monitress came in and in Mlle Verkhovsky's place led us to the dining-room, where the Principal made an immediate appearance. Without going into explanations, 'Maman' spoke only one agitated sentence: 'Children, I trust that you will discuss this deplorable incident neither among yourselves nor with your relatives.' Obviously uncertain what else to say, she looked at us in a bewildered manner and, pressing her hands to her forehead as she always did during the migraines to which she was such a martyr, left the room.

'But what mustn't we talk about? What's happened?' asked the girls who had not yet heard the news.

'So you don't know?' cried Mlle Tufayev: 'We won't have any more of these despicable tricks. You've been taken away from your wretched homes in the back of beyond, looked after and cared for from charity, and this is how you repay your benefactors!'

Choking with fury, she went on: 'You can get this into your thick heads: from now on the sickroom is strictly out of bounds and you must not on any account go anywhere near that nasty little creature.'

Fanny was put to bed as soon as she was caught by the porter, trembling as violently as if she had a fever. Mlle

133

Verkhovsky, the Principal, and even the Directress came to her bedside; so did Mlle Tufayev, who considered it her business to poke her nose in everywhere. Fanny screamed and fainted at the sight of her. The Directress asked the doctor to be summoned to bring her round; but at that moment the girl's mother and uncle, who had been told what had happened, came in and Mme Golembiovsky fell sobbing to her knees at the side of the bed.

With an expression of disgust the Directress pointed imperiously to the sick child and demanded with a slow and careful stress on each syllable: 'I beg of you to relieve me of your shameless daughter without further delay.'

Fanny's mother jumped up as if stung. Looking straight at the Directress she cried furiously: 'There is nothing my daughter has to be ashamed of in running away from the regimentation of the Institute. The shame is Smolny's that a child should have to run away.' And she added that whatever the Directress might say she had no intention of removing her daughter from the sickroom until the doctor guaranteed that it would not endanger her health.

All this time the Directress, so we heard, stood with eyes upraised to heaven (or at least the ceiling) to indicate how far it was beneath her exalted position to take any notice of this impertinent speech; but Mlle Tufayev rushed furiously upon Mme Golembiovsky.

'How dare you speak to our beloved Directress in this way?' she screamed, stamping her foot. 'Do you realize, you miserable creature, that she is held in high regard by the entire Royal Family?' But at this moment the doctor intervened and asked the Directress's permission to have a word with her in private. He must have told her that the girl could not be moved, since for the rest of the day the Directress did not enter the sick girl's room.

Fanny regained consciousness, but only briefly; soon she

developed a high fever, then became delirious, and eventually lay in the sickroom for over a month, during which her mother never left her bedside. Thin even before her illness, Fanny wasted away like a melting candle.

Our Principal, who visited the sick girl more frequently than anyone else, was often in tears at the poor child's side; but at such times, afraid no doubt of what Mlle Tufayev might say, she clutched at her forehead and complained of migraine.

As soon as she grew a little better, Fanny was taken away from the Institute by her mother. A month later a middle-aged woman, some relative of Fanny's, came into our dormitory asking for the return of the girl's box, which had been left behind. Fanny, she told us, had died a few days previously from a galloping consumption.

7

Classroom Desperado

Several months went by and I still could not get used to the life at Smolny. Strict discipline, cold buildings, early rising and continuous hunger made our existence at the Institute extremely hard. The worst thing of all was going to bed, for the dormitories were almost completely unheated. Our nightdresses were so low-cut that they practically fell off our shoulders, and night jackets could only be worn on doctor's orders. We would dive into bed shivering and then be unable to get warm; a sheet and a light blanket worn thin with long use offered poor protection from the cold, and the flimsy mattresses were so much the worse for wear that, when you turned over, the frame of the bed stuck into you and woke you up.

Getting up in the morning was even harder. As soon as the bell sounded at six o'clock, those on duty ran along the line of beds pulling the blankets off and shouting to the girls to hurry up and get dressed. Groans and cries answered them but we got up and dressed by lamplight in a dormitory which had become ice-cold during the night.

Although morning prayers started at seven, the hour which this gave us for dressing was still not enough; our uniform was so absurd that hardly anyone could manage it herself. Help was needed to fasten the dress at the back, pin up the apron, tie the sleeves tidily over the arms, plait the hair into two tight plaits and loop them over the back of the head, and to pin a bow in the middle. Most girls had been taught to dress themselves and do their own hair by the time they came to the Institute, but they soon forgot. This happened in my own case; at home I had managed quite well by myself, but now I was always having to ask my friends to fasten a pin or hold a sleeve-tape or pin my bow.

On top of the torment of early rising came our constant hunger. The food they gave us was quite tasteless and the portions minute. For lunch we might have a small slice of bread with grated cheese or sometimes a paper-thin slice of meat. This miserable dish represented the first course; the second would be a saucer of milk gruel or macaroni. For dinner we had soup, with tiny pieces of meat from it fried for the second course, and for pudding a little pastry with cranberry or some kind of jam. In the morning and evening we had a mug of tea and half a roll.

The various Lents utterly exhausted us: it must have been the Institute's aim to turn us into expert fasters. We fasted not only before Christmas and Easter but every Wednesday and Friday as well. On these days we had three sprats apiece instead of meat, or a few potatoes and salad oil. At fast-times we went to bed in tears, and whimpered restlessly from cold and hunger for quite a time.

One year this hunger resulted in more than half of us having to be taken to the sickroom during the Long Lent. The doctor said he could not take any more girls who were ill, and said quite plainly that inadequate diet was to blame. Through the pupils' relatives the whole town heard what had happened, and a special committee was set up which reached the same conclusions as the doctor. Despite herself the Directress was forced to shorten the length of the fasts; before Easter we now only fasted for three weeks, and before

Christmas two. Wednesdays and Fridays, however, remained as before.

Those of us with relatives in St. Petersburg suffered less than the rest; our visitors would be asked for bread and other food rather than sweets, and also for money which could be secreted. The lucky ones—we called them 'money-bags'— could fortify themselves with food from home and then sit preparing their lessons with their fingers stuffed in their ears, while the other girls wandered about like drowsy flies and gathered into groups to discuss how they could 'organize' some bread or borrow some money.

A girl might be having a music lesson, in which case her mother would have sent her some money to pay for it: realizing the fact, two girls might try to get round her. The money was in her exercise-book and had to be given to the teacher that day, and they would try to persuade her that nothing awful would happen if she apologized to the teacher and said that she would get the money in a few days' time. But no, the teacher might report her to the form-mistress, who would undoubtedly ask her mother to be more careful in her payments another time. . . .

'You're just greedy, that's all! Greedy-guts, that's what we'll all call you after this!' The cadgers start to run off, but their victim is so frightened by their threats that she runs after them and gives them the money.

The pair of them then go downstairs to look for the care-taker. 'Ivan, darling, will you do something for us?' they ask as they fasten on to him and try to keep a good lookout at the same time.

'It's all very well asking', he grumbles, 'but you haven't paid me for the last lot of bread yet.'

'We'll pay you today, Ivan, but will you get what's on this list for us?'

'You needn't give me any list, it's not the first time you've bothered me. Sausage, biscuits, bread and rolls . . . just say what you want to spend and how much I get for my trouble; it's no use putting down the prices of everything, the shops all know I'm not supposed to do this and they charge three times the proper price.'

The girls hurriedly slip him the money and ask him to put the purchases inside the empty stove on the upper corridor.

'Not likely, I'm not going round feeling the stoves. If you're as hungry as all that, you can fetch the stuff: I'll put it under the bench in the lower corridor, and that's that.'

This was his usual place, and as the lower corridor was strictly out of bounds to us coffee-drops, fetching the food had to be entrusted to the desperadoes in return for a share in it.

We needed money for other things as well as food. Although the regulations laid down that pupils were supplied with all the necessities, in actual fact we had to spend a considerable sum each year on combs, toothbrushes, soap and other toilet equipment. Another point was that the purchases were usually entrusted to the form-mistresses, who expected us to buy the most expensive items without the least regard to our resources.

'Children,' Mlle Verkhovsky would say, 'I am going shopping today: does anyone need anything?'

There would be requests for gloves, a brush or soap.

'What sort of soap?'

'Oh, the ordinary, about fifteen kopecks.'

'How can you bear to use such stuff? I'll get you some for sixty kopecks.'

'But then I shall only have one rouble left,' the girl protests timidly, 'and it'll be three months before I get any more money from home.'

Mlle Verkhovsky is well aware of this, since the pupils' money is kept by the form-mistress; but she declares with an expression of disgust:

'I can buy the fifteen-kopeck stuff if you really want me to, I suppose. If I remember correctly it is used for washing clothes; no doubt it will smell quite rancid.'

'Oh well then, Mademoiselle, please buy whatever you think best,' the girl corrects herself hurriedly, afraid of annoying the mistress or appearing mean.

Our maids cost us a lot, as well. Each dormitory had a maid who was supposed to clean it and the form-mistress's room; she swept and dusted but we had to do our own beds and lockers. If there was no time for this before we had to leave for the classroom, or if it was done carelessly, a girl could be scolded and punished: the maid might come to the rescue when she noticed one's things were untidy, but only if one gave her tips. Despite the fact that we all tipped the maid the form-mistress made a collection for her twice a year, and if a maid got married it meant a further big expense for us.

It was the Institute's fault that the gap between children and parents widened and deepened. Girls were not allowed home on holiday or for the summer and so gradually forgot their homes and families; their love for their parents grew weaker and misunderstandings became more frequent. During our long years at the Institute we never once caught a glimpse of wide fields, the sea, rivers and lakes, sunrise and sunset, mountains and forest. Apart from portraits of the Royal Family we had no pictures—no landscapes, not even portraits of great writers: we were not even allowed to pin pictures of our family above our beds. It was this kind of regimentation which drove the humanity from those who went to Smolny.

How a girl from a poor family would blush if she had to sit beside a dowdily-dressed mother or sister on reception days! And her embarrassment was worse when a form-mistress deliberately came up and spoke to the mother in

French, which she could not understand. Sometimes a girl might tell not only her form-mistress but her friends that the poorly-dressed woman who had visited her on Sunday had been not her mother but her nurse.

Artificial emotions had to be invented to take the place of genuine feeling. There was the business of 'adoration'; girls would 'adore' priests, masters and deacons and the coffee-drops even adored the older pupils. A girl who encountered the object of her adoration would shout 'my adored one!'; 'my wonderful one!' or might kiss the loved one's shoulder. A girl punished for being so overcome by excitement that she stepped out of line considered herself lucky at suffering for her idol. The more daring adorers went down to the lower corridor and poured scent on to their loved ones' clothes, or snipped bits from their coats that they could keep pressed to their bosom. Some went so far as to scratch their loved ones' initials on their own arms with a heated needle or a pen-knife; but mercifully such martyrs were few.

The form-mistresses did not penalize us for indulging in this adoration; on the contrary Mlle Verkhovsky, the young-est and best-looking one, was perfectly happy to listen to our expressions of delight. Before leaving the Institute on her day off she would open the door of her room and, gaily dressed and smiling, ask us how we liked her clothes. Such informality was rare and we would crowd round at once and tell her how wonderful she looked; and, flattered by such admiration, she would float out with her pretty head proudly uplifted.

It took me the whole of my first year at Smolny to get used to the early rising, the hunger, the cold, the grim bare walls and the regimentation of the Institute's system. I found myself trembling with fever and coughed so badly that at night I woke up the other girls and in the daytime inter-rupted the lessons; I always felt half-asleep and went about dull and listless as I mechanically did what I was told. But the staff decided I was an obedient child and were actually kind to me, sending me to the sickroom whenever they thought I looked ill.

The sickroom provided my only relief and consolation; it was warmer, the food was better, and one could sleep. I even liked the fact that the attendants called each other by their christian names, just like people outside. Freed from hunger and cold I used to fall sound asleep and wake up the next day perfectly recovered; and the doctor, well aware that my illness was the product of a poor diet and over-austere conditions, was never in a hurry to send me back to the classroom. I was usually perfectly happy until the arrival of new patients, whom I could only regard as enemies.

Within a few hours of leaving the sickroom I would be feverish and drowsy again. If this happened when we were preparing something I made myself a bed between the benches, using some textbooks covered with a cape as my pillow. I lay on the floor at my friends' feet, and as they worked they would throw down scarves to me so that I could cover myself up and go to sleep. The duty-mistress looked in at intervals but could not see me; if she did happen to remember my existence a girl kicked me and I jumped up as though nothing had happened, and said if she asked where I had sprung from that I was looking for a book I had dropped.

During my early years at Smolny my uncle and his wife used to visit me. My uncle was a general of some importance and had various orders and medals including a diamond star on his chest, and his wife was always beautifully dressed. They came in a smart carriage with a manservant at the back; while they sat in the Institute's reception room he stood loaded with their coats in the anteroom.

Knowing how much wealth and rich living were valued

at the Institute, I was very proud of my important relatives; but of my own mother I now thought with increasing irritation. Every year she sent me four or five roubles and I had to let her know as soon as it arrived. I answered not through the form-mistress but in letters which my friends' relatives posted for me. This is what I said in a letter I found when I eventually returned home:

'Dear Mother, I must ask you not to bother to send me the four or five roubles a year. It is not enough to buy soap, combs and brushes—let alone replace the regulation shoes which fall off our feet during dancing lessons. The money will not even buy a pair of gloves for me to wear at the Institute balls, which I attend not because I enjoy them but because I have to; the tattered old gloves I take after my friends have thrown them away merely make me a laughing-stock. I cannot order a corset with what you send me but have to make do with the school one which leaves me covered in scratches and bruises. In order to make a few extra roubles I sew capes and aprons for my friends. The girls whose mothers love them are sent money not only for the essentials but for them to get the maids to do their sewing. So you see, Mother, what you let me have is no use here so please don't bother to send me four or even five roubles.'

Twice a year, at Christmas and Easter, we had a ball. Unfortunately the entire staff was present but no one from outside was invited and the girls had to dance together. Sitting in a long row of chairs placed along one wall the Directress, the Principal and the form-mistresses never took their eyes off them the whole evening. The plain girls and those who were in the staff's bad books tried to keep as far away as possible. Laughing and joking and playing the fool were strictly forbidden; many of us would rather have stayed away but everybody without exception had to make an appearance. The ghastly tedium of these balls was only bearable as far as we were concerned because after the dance we were each given two veal sandwiches, some crystallized fruit and a pastry.

Our sole entertainment consisted of a walk in the Tavrichesky Gardens, which took place once a year in the summer. Although during our ceremonious procession from Smolny to Tavrichesky the porter and the other servants drove off everyone we encountered *en route*, and although we saw no one in the gardens apart from our own staff and pupils—they were closed to the public on the day we went—we loved the walk and looked forward to the great day with impatience. For two or three hours we walked along the avenues and lawns of a garden which was not our own, and might even catch a distant glimpse of an unfamiliar face or see a carriage flash by; and as we walked through the streets there might be a chance of slowing down by a shop-window or turning round to look at a passer-by. All this made so deep an impression on the prisoners of Smolny nunnery that every detail of the walk would be a subject for discussion for months afterward.

In the junior class the form-mistress was a Mlle Nechayev. She was really quite unbalanced—always shouting at her 'coffee-drops' and throwing books at them and standing them in the corner for hours on end. Sobbing and whimpering could always be heard coming from her dormitory and her girls would arrive in the classroom and dining-room with their eyes swollen with tears. Before long she began to give way to fresh outbursts; in the middle of the night she would run down the dormitory shouting to the girls to get up. She would pull off their blankets, grab them by the arms and call to them in piercing tones: 'Start to pray, the Lord is angry with you!'—and she would make the children throw themselves down beside her in their nightdresses on the cold floor.

Classroom Desperado

Once she roused her girls and dragged them to the class-room without giving them time to dress. An army of bare-foot 'coffee-drops' ran sobbing after her down the long corridors and staircases. After prayers in the classroom they were led to the Principal's apartments. The Principal had been perfectly aware even before this that Mlle Nechayev treated her charges appallingly and was in the habit of waking them up after they had gone to bed, but she had shut her eyes to it: only now, when the half-clad children were brought to her in the middle of the night, did she decide to take action. The next day a doctor was called in. He pronounced Mlle Nechayev insane and had her sent to a lunatic asylum.

Among the form-mistresses only Mlle Verkhovsky had a slightly different outlook; she alone considered it her duty to explain the lessons to her pupils, talk to them about various things and encourage them to read.

She had a very uneven temperament. In a good mood she seemed kind, charming and intelligent; we could stroll freely about our enormous dormitory, talking loudly and even laughing happily from time to time. Then we might pluck up our courage and send someone to ask: 'Please, Mlle Verkhovsky, would you read to us?' The request was promptly taken up by other voices and in a few minutes the entire dormitory was chanting various versions of the same plea. At last the door opened and Mlle Verkhovsky emerged with a charming smile to read us *Pickwick Papers* or some-thing of the sort. These readings which we enjoyed so thor-oughly sometimes went on every day for a month or more, much to our delight.

But then everything altered as suddenly as though at the wave of a wand. Mlle Verkhovsky was subject to fits of temper which made her unbearable; at these times we were more afraid of her than any of the other form-mistresses. We dared not move, turned over the pages of our textbooks

with care, and saw that a deathly silence reigned in the
dormitory.

It was a holiday, and after dinner we went into our dormitory. Mlle Verkhovsky announced that she was free, called us
into her room, threw a handful of nuts and sweets to everyone and told us to sit down. The form-mistresses' rooms
were not very large, and we had to sit on the floor as well as
the chairs and sofa, but we crowded round her and begged
her to tell us a story. We did not have to wait long.

Chewing sweets and cracking nuts we laughed aloud as
she recounted an amusing scene from a play she had been to
when the door suddenly opened and Mlle Tufayev appeared.

'How very touching,' she observed with a sneer. 'You *do*
enjoy their adoration, don't you? But of course you're still
very young. . . . Personally I am quite indifferent to both their
adoration and their hatred.'

'I wasn't under the impression I had done anything against
the rules,' said Mlle Verkhovsky with a blush.

Mlle Tufayev looked at her over the top of her spectacles,
drew herself up, and replied in a voice which already betrayed
her annoyance and displeasure: 'I doubt whether molly-
coddling the girls like this is allowed; no one permits them
such familiarities but you. However, it is possible of course
that the Directress may approve: I shall have to inquire.'

She left the room, and Mlle Verkhovsky tried to pretend
that nothing had happened. She shrugged her shoulders
lightly and picked up a book; but when she read it was
without expression and her mind was obviously elsewhere.
After a minute or two she said with an assumed calm: 'I have
some letters to write; will you go back to your room?'

We went into our dormitory and gathered in the far
corner where she could not hear our conversation.

'It might blow over,' somebody whispered. 'Some hope!'

replied another. Even the pious suggestion that we should all kneel before the icons and repeat twelve times 'Lord, remember David and all his trouble'—usually considered an infallible antidote—was ignored: we were all much too alarmed.

Suddenly a monitress ran in, knocked on Mlle Verkhovsky's door, and said that the Directress wished to see her. We gathered from her knitted brows and compressed lips when she returned that the storm had broken. After tea and prayers she went straight to her room without a word to us and slammed the door hard behind her. It was a relief to find she was not going to stay with us and we had hopes that her temper would cool down overnight and the storm would pass over.

The next morning, however, she was still like a thundercloud when she got up; and she announced that although she was not on duty she intended to stay in and give us extra lessons in the evening.

When we got back to the dormitory after dinner she merely said that she had promised the French master to make us conjugate our verbs. She was pale and kept pressing her forehead as though she had a headache.

We arranged ourselves on two benches by the table and began conjugating in turn; partly because we did not know them properly and partly because we were scared of her grim and angry expression we kept making mistakes.

'Blockheads, idiots!' she shouted at us furiously. She pushed one girl so hard that she knocked her head against the wall, tore the apron off another, and sent several out of the room. Then my turn came.

'What? What? Start again!' she shouted with an angry stamp of the foot.

Completely confused, I relapsed into silence and could only look down and pull at my apron with trembling fingers.

'You knew this verb when you conjugated it for me the other day: what are you doing, deliberately trying to make a fool of me?' She rose from her chair and pulled my arm so that the pain made me cry out.

The bell went and Mlle Verkhovsky told the others to go to the dining-room; me she pushed into the corner with such force that I fell on to my knees. She went to her room but returned a moment later with an angry flush in her cheeks. With shaking hands she clutched me by the shoulders, dragged me from my knees and to the accompaniment of a stream of abuse began to tear off my apron and frock. 'You little wretch, you sleep all through the year and when I try to help you to catch up with the others this is the gratitude I get! What nasty mean creatures you all are. . . .'

I tore myself away and ran screaming to the door, but she caught hold of me, dragged me to her room and turned the key in the lock. Then she picked up a length of rope and began to rain blows on my head and shoulders and face.

Probably I should have had a severe thrashing had not we heard from downstairs the noise of the girls getting up from table. Mlle Verkhovsky threw down the rope and thrust a jug of water and a towel at me, presumably so that I could wipe my face; but I threw the jug on the floor and shouted tearfully: 'I'll tell everybody what happened, I'll write home about it. . . . You've no right to beat us like this!'

When the girls came back to the dormitory I told them tearfully what had happened, deliberately shouting at the top of my voice so that Mlle Verkhovsky should hear; but my throat was so constricted with sobs that only occasional words were audible. Then I rushed across the room and threw myself on my knees before the icons and vowed from that moment on to be a 'desperado'; I would answer back and argue with all the mistresses and be as impertinent as I could, especially to that 'wild beast'. My friends crowded round and listened to my oath with bated breath, secretly approving my daring.

From then on I was indeed a 'desperado'. Mlle Verkhovsky, who had heard every word, now avoided me. She disregarded me completely, bothering neither to ask me questions, tell me when I went wrong, nor call me to see her—and thus never gave me a chance to be rude to her. But I took every opportunity to be rude to Mlle Tufayev.

'You're not allowed to pull our arms,' I would cheekily protest if she hauled us up to stand by the blackboard for talking too loudly.

'Stand by that board for two hours!' she would order me; but I would look her straight in the eye and say: 'I'll tell the mistress tomorrow that you did not let me do her preparation.'

The girls expected a lot from us desperadoes and I was punished practically every day. The attitude of the staff towards me changed completely and they pounced on me for the slightest thing; then again, my friends were always making life difficult for me by taking advantage of the fact that I was a desperado. 'Do go down to the lower corridor and ask the caretaker to buy some bread for me,' one of my friends would say.

'But Mlle Tufayev has only just gone downstairs!'

'Jolly fine desperado you are if you're scared to do anything!' and, quaking with fright but determined not to show it, I would start on my perilous journey.

I was always being caught and so came in for a great deal of abuse and punishment. At night I often wept at the thought of my unhappy lot and the difficulties of being a desperado, but I never forgot my oath.

Meanwhile the days at the Institute, as monotonously identical as so many drops of water, passed unnoticed. I moved up from the coffee-drops' class into the senior form but it made little difference to me apart from the fact that we all wore green frocks instead of brown and the mistresses did not pull us about so much.

One was a junior for three years and a senior for another three, during which time new subjects were taught us including—for they wanted to make good managers of us— the culinary art. We went to the kitchen in groups of five or six and, under the supervision of the cook, embarked on cooking. The kitchen provided us with splendid entertainment so these classes were always popular. They meant that we spent so much less time on our boring lessons and for several hours escaped the supervision of a mistress.

Like everything else we were taught at Smolny, these culinary lessons were of little practical value. By the time we made our appearance in the kitchen everything was laid on a table; a lump of meat, ready-mixed dough, potatoes in a basin, a few root vegetables, sugar. We never did see how the dough was prepared, did not know what cut of beef lay before us, and could not fry rissoles. The cook regarded our studies as a bit of fun which had been allowed the young ladies; afraid that we might burn our hands or let the rissoles spoil she prepared the soup herself and personally put the pans on the stove. We were told to crush the sugar, cut out the dough for pastry, chop the vegetables and peel the potatoes—all of which we thoroughly enjoyed. We sang as we peeled and chopped meat and vegetables to the rhythm of a Russian dance. The gay mood of the kitchen was also partly due to the fact that we were allowed to eat anything we had prepared with our own hands—an extremely important point in view of our perpetual hunger.

Girls who could embroider carpets or do satin stitching were always busy. We were for ever embroidering trimmings for capes and towels at Smolny, but the carpets were for presents on such occasions as the Directress's name-day or some anniversary on which something or other had to be presented to a member of the staff. As the actual needlework lessons were quite useless when it came to making one of these presents, the teacher would ask our form-mistresses to let us come into the needlework room in the evenings; sometimes girls spent their entire evening embroidering a carpet instead of doing their lessons. When the present was for somebody really important the Principal even allowed the needlework mistress to take us away from our ordinary lessons if the evenings were not enough, and a number of girls might be absent from class work for weeks or even months on end.

French was considered the most important subject at the Institute and in every class the majority of the hours were spent on the subject. We were supposed to speak French even among ourselves, and if a mistress heard us using our own language she would shout: 'How dare you talk in Russian?' Since, however, there were no books available to us in either Russian or French, our progress was none the less poor.

The uncivilized behaviour of our mistresses turned us into uncouth creatures too. We quarrelled until the swear-words poured out of us like water from a jug and it never entered our heads to treat each other with any consideration or pay regard to other people's feelings. Often we would gather to make lists of which girls were beautiful and which were ugly, and then shout in their faces: 'You're top of the class for beauty. You get top marks for ugliness. You come second in stupidity.'

One day my uncle wrote saying that my younger brother Zarya had graduated and was stationed in St. Petersburg with the Dvoryansky Regiment, and he promised to bring him along to see me on the next reception day.

These reception days for relatives were held twice a week

—on Sunday afternoons from one till four, and on Thursday evenings from six till eight. Girls who were expecting relatives strolled about in pairs in the ballroom and those whose relatives had already arrived sat with them on benches round the walls. There were always monitresses and duty-mistresses walking around.

My uncle came marching into the room with a young man in uniform behind him: when he looked at me I realized it was my brother Zarya, and somewhat to my own surprise a warm wave of affection replaced my usual indifference. Quite forgetting the regulations I threw myself in tears into my brother's arms.

After a minute or two when I had calmed down my uncle remarked to Zarya: 'Of course adoration is a pastime here, you know. Why, they even adore the caretakers and the men who clean the lamps!'

I felt so insulted I began to explain with some pride that we never adored anybody lower than a deacon at Smolny, whatever else might go on at other institutes.

'This is wonderful!' cried Uncle with a roar of laughter. 'Do tell us how you adore people!'

I started to recount the terms used on the object of one's adoration and how scent might be poured over a master's coat and hat. 'You see that girl there?' I whispered, pointing out a pupil sitting not far away. 'She adores the art master, and he has a big dirty-looking wart on his forehead and marks under his nose from always taking snuff.'

'But why do you adore such frightful-looking people?'

Amazed at such a question, I explained that they were all that was available at Smolny.

Uncle couldn't let the matter end there. 'And how do you show your adoration for the priest?' he inquired.

'Well, instead of the ordinary coloured egg at Eastertime he is given beautifully embroidered ones made of silk; and

before the ceremony of kissing him three times after the
service you rub your lips with scent.'

'How stupid all this is, how vulgar and absurd!' interrupted
my brother, who had been silent up to this point. His attitude
annoyed my uncle very much; thinking him unnecessarily
serious he started teasing his nephew for his unmilitary tendency to spend day and night poring over books. He told
him he must not try to ram education down his sister's
throat as so many young men did. 'It's wrong to make a
girl into a blue-stocking,' he concluded.

I pacified him by saying that I wasn't fond of reading and
that in any case the authorities were more interested in how
we behaved than in what we learned. 'Quite right too!' he
exclaimed.

My brother said nothing but looked round him vaguely;
in an attempt to clear the atmosphere my uncle changed the
subject.

'Whoever's that?' he inquired, pointing to Mlle Tufayev.
'She looks a proper toad!'

I leant over and explained that she was a form-mistress,
adding that if anyone overheard him I should be in terrible
trouble with my superiors.

'Superiors? So she's your superior?'; but Uncle changed
his tone. Although his eyes still betrayed his amusement he
said with a severe shake of the finger: 'You watch out.
There's nothing so important as a respect for authority. And
make sure that no one ever has a bad word for you.'

As soon as my uncle had gone and left us together, Zarya
said that it was all very well for rich girls such as Uncle's
daughters to rely on good behaviour; it wouldn't do a poor
girl like me any harm to acquire a little knowledge. His
words reminded me of the lectures on poverty which Mother
was always reading us children: at the Institute I had made
every effort to forget our condition, and had very nearly

succeeded until my brother reminded me of it the very first moment he set foot in the Institute after I had not seen him for so many years. The feeling of affection for him that had come over me vanished and I continued talking to him without enthusiasm. Now, however, he began showering me with questions; he asked what we did in literature, and I answered with pride that Lermontov took up eighteen pages in our textbook and Pushkin a whole thirty-two. From what I said he realized that I had not in fact read a single one of their works.

'What a fool you must have for a master!' said Zarya sadly. 'You don't seem to have learned anything here except how to adore.'

This I could not let pass. 'Not everybody is of the same opinion,' I said condescendingly. 'Our Institute is acknowledged everywhere to be the first in Russia, and Starov our Russian master is a famous poet whom even such "fools" as our form-mistresses recognize."

'There is no such famous poet in Russia, and your form-mistresses recognize him precisely because they *are* fools.'

This was too much, and I jumped up intending to run off without saying good-bye; but Zarya caught my hands just in time. He spoke at some length very tenderly asking me to forgive him, and ended up by saying that I must read and he would bring me some books. This offer I refused categorically, saying that I had so much routine work I never had a free minute.

Seeing that I still wanted to be rid of him, my brother changed the subject. Mother was longing to come to St. Petersburg for the day of my graduation from the Institute, he said, and had been putting a few roubles by every month for a long time to save up for it.

'What a pointless sacrifice!' I could not help saying.

'Pointless?' repeated my brother with surprise. 'What do

you mean? Don't you want to see your own mother after all this time?'

'Of course I do, but not if it's so difficult for her. I'm sure Uncle would have me at his place, please persuade her I shall be all right and that it really isn't necessary for her to come.'

Deducing nothing from my chatter but the fact that I did not want Mother to fetch me, he started to try and discover why: without realizing there was anything discreditable in my reasons I told him everything.

'Not everybody believes that poverty is something to be proud of,' I said sarcastically. 'If Mother does come to fetch me I suppose she'll turn up in the same dress that was made when she brought me here. Do you imagine I shall enjoy having everyone laugh at the way she dresses?'

'That's enough!' said my brother suddenly, pushing back his chair. 'Is that the kind of thing they teach you here?': and, red in the face, he went out without saying good-bye.

My depression deepened when I read the letter from Sasha, my favourite sister, which Zarya had given me during our disastrous meeting; she sent it through him instead of by post as she did not want it read by a form-mistress as was done with our ordinary letters.

Sasha's letter profoundly shook me. When I could stop crying I re-read the sheet covered with the familiar hand-writing:

'My dear girl, my own darling sister: I beg you by all you still hold holy—the memory of our dear departed Nanny, the affection you once had for me and which still brings tears to my eyes when I think of it—to take a hold on yourself and try to melt your frozen heart with thoughts of those who are near to you. Pull yourself together, my dear, and tell me why you have broken with us all so ruthlessly and what has happened at the Institute to alter you so much? Why have you become so stony-hearted as your letters to

Mother suggest? Once upon a time you used to be so open with me, couldn't you try now to give me a really honest answer so that we could work out together the best way of helping you to overcome whatever has upset you so much?

'I should also be interested to hear how your work is going, what subjects particularly interest you, what you are reading, and what your dreams and ambitions are and what you plan to do when you leave.'

I tore up several letters before I eventually sent off an answer, feeling for the first time that I was completely incapable of expressing myself. Finally I wrote a letter consisting of short confused sentences:

'Sasha darling: do you remember you used to tell me a story about a poor girl? When she was born the fairy who turned up had already given away all her nicest presents that day—wealth, beauty and happiness. She gave her the only thing she had left—tears. Well, there was a fairy at my cradle too, a cross old thing who only shouted "Topsy-turvy, that's what you'll be all your life, topsy-turvy". The wicked fairy's words came true and with me everything always turns out wrong.

'I swear in God's name I am telling you the truth. I set out to do one thing and end up by doing something completely different. I had no intention of deceiving you when I promised I would work hard and behave well: things just turned out differently. Sometimes I think that if I wasn't always so hungry and cold it wouldn't have happened this way. I'm sorry to talk about these mundane matters to anyone as far above them as you. But what can I do when hunger and cold tear my inside to pieces as I go to bed? Perhaps it isn't that, though. I don't know why everything is so depressing.

'My conduct is pretty awful. When I was still in the "coffee-drops" Mlle Verkhovsky, my form-mistress, went for me quite unfairly. She gave me a thrashing but I was more upset by her anger and so I swore in front of the icon before the whole dormitory that I would become a "desperado". And I'm still keeping my oath. I answer all the form-mistresses back and I'm cheeky and I argue and do all the dares I'm asked to. All this has put me in the staff's bad books; the mistresses chorus that I ought to be expelled. I'm sure you realize, Sasha, that I cannot stop being a desperado: I took an oath before the icon, and if I stop my friends will think I am trying to suck up to the staff. . . . But if only you knew how awful it is to be a desperado! I hate it so much, but of course I have to hide the fact from my friends. Oh, Sasha, the whole thing is so depressing, so depressing.

'You ask what my dreams are: only that you would visit me, just for one day, just for one hour, even. I would put my head in your lap and you would stroke my hair and I would cry and cry and cry until I felt better. . . . Sasha, my adored best-beloved sister: don't take this as rudeness, but I implore you not to write to me any more if you cannot come and see me. Your letters are a torture to me, they break my heart. I'm horrible, I know, but I beg you on my knees: forgive me, and do try to love me just a little.'

One day Zarya told me he would be too busy to visit me for three or four weeks, so on the next few reception days I sat by myself in the dormitory instead of going down to the ballroom; but half an hour before the end of visiting hours a monitress looked in and said that someone had come to see me.

I ran happily down the stairs and was about to enter the ballroom when I was stopped by Mlle Tufayev asking who my visitors were.

'I expect it's my brother who had been coming to see me all this winter and my uncle,' I said.

'You are not expecting anyone else?'

'Oh, no,' I answered, and ran off without noticing that she was following.

There were a lot of people at the entrance to the ballroom, some of them having said good-bye and on the point of leaving. I saw my brother and began to make my way towards him when I realized with some surprise that he was not alone.

'May I introduce a great friend of mine?' said Zarya, indicating the handsome young officer who was standing beside him.

Slightly embarrassed, I curtsied.

The officer clicked his heels and said: 'I have heard a great deal about the strict discipline of your Institute, but I was so eager to meet my best friend's sister that under his protection I have dared to penetrate into the Nunnery.'

Not knowing what answer to make, I curtsied again without lifting my eyes.

Suddenly the officer laughed and stretched out his hands to me. 'Lisa,' he cried, 'don't you really recognize me?'

I looked up. There before me stood my elder brother Andrei, altered and grown beyond recognition. I gasped and threw myself on his neck.

'My darling sister,' he asked as he hugged and kissed me, 'have I really changed so much?'

I defended myself by saying that he really had altered a good deal since I had seen him five and a half years previously when, just before I entered the Institute, he had been posted to a regiment in one of the nearby provinces: and in any case I had never expected to see him at Smolny.

Although we had spent so little time together, I was so delighted at having met Andrei that I went back to the dormitory beaming with happiness: but on the threshold Mlle Tufayev stopped me, her face contorted with rage. She pointed at me and shouted at the top of her voice: 'No one is to speak to this filthy creature or go anywhere near her: she has disgraced our noble institution!'

'Who? I have?' I murmured looking round, unable to believe my ears and not realizing what was happening.

'Stop acting!' shrieked Mlle Tufayev, spluttering with indignation. 'Oh, no, my lady—you know perfectly well that you're the bane of the entire Institute. This time, thank goodness, we shall get rid of you for good.'

Then she turned to the girls who had practically hemmed us in and shouted: 'I had it from her own lips, her very own lips, that she was expecting her uncle and her brother, both of whom we know perfectly well, and yet her brother—I heard this with my own ears—her *brother* pointed to an officer he had brought with him and introduced him as his friend. The officer said he had been afraid to penetrate our strict Institute and had only risked doing so under the protection of her brother—what do you think of that?'

Mlle Tufayev surveyed the girls in triumph for a moment before continuing: 'This wretched creature contented herself with curtsying to him at first and then she decided not to restrain herself and she . . . words fail me . . . she actually *threw* herself on his neck! I myself watched them with my very eyes kissing each other passionately over and over again! Oh!'—Mlle Tufayev was almost moaning by this time—'I saw every detail of it, I was standing just behind them all the time!'

'It was my elder brother!' I shouted. 'I hadn't seen him for over five years and I didn't recognize him at first. Then, when I did . . .'

'Silence!' screamed Mlle Tufayev. 'You dirty creature, you filthy slut!' and she called me by all the swear-words she knew in both French and Russian. Then she came right up to me, stamped her foot, and said: 'We'll see what the Directress has to say about all this'—and ran from the room.

The moment the door shut behind her the girls came crowding round. No one doubted that I had spoken the truth: to kiss a strange man in public—in visiting hours, of all times!—was unthinkable at the Institute. Some tried to cheer me up by saying that the authorities would never believe such a slander; but others were afraid the Directress might be ready, because of my activities as a desperado, to expel me from the Institute.

Suddenly the door was flung open and the Principal came in accompanied by Mlle Tufayev.

'You miserable creature!' exclaimed 'Maman'. 'How dared you do such a terrible thing!'

'It's not true, Maman—I swear in God's name it is a slander,' I sobbed. 'Mlle Tufayev has always had a down on me.'

'How dare you speak about a respected member of the staff like that!'

Then all my friends surrounded the Principal and all cried at once: 'Maman, Maman, it was her brother—she did not recognize him at first!'

'Silence!' ordered Mlle Tufayev: and turning to the Principal she said: 'Now you see, Madame, the immoral influence she has on the others; they even interrupt *you*.'

At that moment the dinner bell rang—just in time, it seemed, to save Maman, who was completely nonplussed. She hurried at once to the door, but before she went out turned to me and said: 'When you have properly considered your disgraceful behaviour and are prepared to apologize for what you have done you may come and see me, but not before.'

'But I can't apologize for something I haven't done,' I said tearfully. 'I swear by all that's holy it was my own brother.'

She looked at me helplessly. Mlle Tufayev turned to the corner where the icon hung: 'And I swear before the icon,

Classroom Desperado

Madame,' she said, 'that everything I have told you is gospel truth. I saw what happened with my own eyes and heard it with my own ears. We shall see whom you are going to believe—me, who has served here faithfully for over thirty-six years, or this little slut, whose own brother introduces to her. . . .'

But Maman was quick to stop her. 'Oh, Mlle Tufayev!' she cried, clutching her forehead, and shut the door hurriedly behind her without saying another word.

The girls formed pairs. When I went up to the girl I always went with Mlle Tufayev rushed up and pulled me by the hand. 'You're not to mix with the others,' she said. 'You must walk by yourself behind the rest of them, all alone, just like a leper.'

'You Judas, you liar, you slanderer!' I yelled, quite beside myself. 'Don't you dare touch me!'

'I shall report all this to the Directress,' hissed Mlle Tufayev.

'Even what didn't happen?' suggested Masha Ratmanov with a loud laugh.

At table I could scarcely swallow anything, despite my hunger: I was too worried thinking about what might happen to me. 'How terrible it would be for Mother if I were expelled,' I told myself. 'It's all up with me now, but at least I shall defend myself with my last drop of blood.' But then my neighbour pressed my foot under the table and slipped a note under my slice of bread. It said: 'You're going to be thrown out in any case: please be so rude to the authorities before you go that the walls crackle.'

'Selfish beasts!' I thought. 'Here am I unjustly disgraced for the rest of my life and instead of feeling sorry for me they only consider their own amusement and won't even let me think what to do.'

On the way back from the dining-room to the dormitory I once more had to walk behind the others. Passing the narrow passage which led to the Principal's rooms I slowed down, but Mlle Tufayev stood right at the entrance as though barring my way. I settled at my desk in the classroom and was beginning to get my books out when she called: 'You needn't bother about lessons. You'll be thrown out in disgrace before long, my treasure, and the reason why will be written down on your certificate. Come here: you can take off that apron and stand by the board until tea-time.'

Silently I did as she said. In the deathly hush Masha Ratmanov observed suddenly: 'It's funny that some people just can't satisfy their malice.'

Mlle Tufayev pretended not to hear: bending over the stocking she was for ever knitting she muttered a few more abuses and then got up and said that we were to sit quietly as she was going to her room for a drink of coffee. As soon as the door closed behind her I took the chalk and wrote on the blackboard: 'In view of what you have said and of your dirty slander I consider myself already expelled from the Institute and therefore do not consider it necessary to subject myself any longer to your tyranny. Elizabeth Tsevlovsky.'

'Bravo, bravo!' shouted Masha; she ran up, seized me round the waist and began to dance me round the classroom. I tore myself away, put on my apron and ran to the Principal.

'Maman,' I cried as I threw myself on my knees before her, 'you are the only one who can save me, you must be my mother now.'

'Dear God,' she answered sadly, 'what can I do? I begged Mlle Tufayev to give us the chance to clear things up by postponing her visit to the Directress for a day or two, but she never listens to what anyone says.'

After a few moments' silence she went on: 'My child, you are the only one who can not only save yourself but also save me from much unpleasantness. Kneel before Mlle Tufayev, not me, and beg her to forgive you for having been so rude and impertinent, and promise her you will really try to behave better. She will be touched. . . . Yes, I am sure she would be deeply touched by your repentance.'

This was too much. I jumped up as if stung; her words seemed to me like an insult. Forgetting the Institute's rules about politeness, and feeling in any case that I had nothing to lose now, I began to say quite fearlessly everything that came into my head.

'You tell me to ask for forgiveness, Maman, but how can I when I do not consider myself guilty of anything that ought to be forgiven? You say I should kneel before someone who is loathed by every girl in the Institute and by me in particular—I'd sooner let myself be torn to pieces!"

Choking with tears, I went on with some difficulty: 'I realize I shall be thrown out of here, but I shall get my own back for this slander. I swear I shall spend my whole life getting my revenge on everybody. I shall get a petition to the Tsar through my uncle, who can always get an audience with him, and my uncle will tell him how young girls are slandered at Smolny and thrown out instead of being looked after!'

The Principal trembled at this and clutched at her forehead in her habitual way, but I could not stop.

'And he'll tell him there is no one here to speak up for us,' I hurried on as though afraid my courage might desert me, 'even you, Maman, whom everyone thinks is so kind and clever, even you are not prepared to speak up for me although you know perfectly well that I am innocent.'

My throat was constricted and, unable to speak for tears, I fell on my knees again before her. Eventually I felt her trembling fingers on my head. Stroking my hair, she said: 'What a little hothead you are! I understand why the staff dislike you so much, my child, and why this could only have happened to you!' And she added with a sigh: 'But as God's my witness there's nothing that I can do, much as I want to.'

And then a good idea came to me: my uncle should be written to at once and asked to explain to the authorities that it really had been my brother who came to see me. I lifted up my tear-stained face and suggested this to the Principal, who hesitated momentarily and then said as though pleased: 'Well, you could write: yes, yes, write by all means, it may be the best solution for us all. I shall send your letter by cab with a maid. But of course you must not say anything rude about Mlle Tufayev.' She sat me at a table, gave me a sheet of paper and left the room.

My letter was brief and to the point: I told my uncle about my brothers' visit and explained why Mlle Tufayev had imagined Andrei had been a total stranger to me. I begged him to clear the matter up the same day, as I had been informed that I was about to be expelled from the Institute for receiving an unknown officer whom I had kissed.

I was finishing the last line when Maman came back. 'You can see now how naïve you are, my child,' she said. 'You think I am all-powerful, but I could not even persuade Mlle Tufayev to wait with this business until tomorrow. She has been to the Directress already.' Then she read my letter carefully, sealed it and gave it to the maid, whom she told to deliver it by cab without losing a moment and to wait for an answer.

A little calmer, I went to my dormitory. My friends told me that Mlle Tufayev had seen my note to her on the blackboard as soon as she returned to the classroom; she read it several times and announced, quivering with rage, that she was going straight to the Directress.

When it was time for tea and the girls went down to the dining-room I went to the Principal's room again and knocked on the door. I had just sat down when the maid returned; my uncle was just going out to his carriage when she had driven up, she told me, but when he took the letter he went back inside. Then he came out again, asked her to inform the Principal he was going straight to the Directress, and told his coachman to start off.

I went out into the corridor to meet my uncle, feeling so nervous that my teeth kept chattering and my throat went dry. I realized that my fate was being decided at this moment, for by my calculations he was already with the Directress. The minutes I counted as I paced up and down the corridor had never seemed so agonizingly long, but at last his heavy tread sounded on the stairs and I ran to meet him.

'What's this nasty business all about?' he asked me sternly.

'Uncle dear, not so loud, somebody will hear,' and he listened with a frown as I hurriedly told him what had happened.

'No, I'm not going to let them get away with this,' he said slowly, adding in my ear: 'I've already trodden on your Directress's tail. That'll make her squeal. Sitting there like an idol. . . . She ought to be in a museum, the old Egyptian mummy, not running an Institute!' And at this he began to laugh until his whole massive body shook.

Hearing his laughter the Principal sent a maid to ask us to see her. When we entered her room she rose and, giving my uncle her hand, said she was delighted he had been able to come so promptly. 'No doubt the whole sad case can now be cleared up,' she said: but my uncle did not let her finish. He was better accustomed to commanding a regiment, to shouting and giving orders, than to making conversation with ladies, and he did not beat about the bush.

'This is not a "sad case", Madame, it is a disgusting business. I have already warned the Directress, and I now have the honour to inform you that I consider it my duty, yes, my duty, to lay the whole matter before His Majesty the Tsar.

'My wife, the respected mother of a family, is the most

peace-loving creature imaginable, but even she was indignant when she read my niece's letter. A decent form-mistress who suspected a pupil of such a crime should, she said, not even have mentioned it to the girl but written straight to me demanding an explanation about the young men who had visited her. Mlle Tufayev, however, did precisely the opposite: she went for my niece straight away and accused her of improper behaviour. Do you realize, Madame, what repercussions this might have had? The whole town would have got to hear about it, mud would have been spattered on me, and the girl's reputation would have been ruined for ever. In the days of the Empress Elizabeth—that wisest of women —such a person as Mlle Tufayev would have had her tongue cut out!'

'General, General . . . Your Excellency!' Maman was horrified. 'We never discuss the staff in front of the pupils like that!'

My uncle wheeled round and shouted at the top of his voice: 'What are you doing here, you scallywag? Just see you show a proper respect for authority in future!'

I shot into the next room like a scalded cat but stayed just behind the door: Uncle's voice could be heard all over the Principal's apartments and I never missed a word of their conversation.

'But where is my guilt in all this?' asked the Principal, feebly trying to justify herself. 'I tried to persuade Mlle Tufayev not to go to the Directress. . . .'

'You, Madame, are guilty on every count, I assure you,' my uncle thundered. 'You are in command here but you have allowed your staff to get completely out of hand. Such unsuitable people should never be employed in the first place, but in any case you should rule your employees with an iron hand so that they haven't even the temerity to squeak, let alone get out of control like this. I regard the matter as very serious. You'll have to excuse me, Madame, I'm a simple Russian soldier, I've been under enemy fire a good many times but I've served my Emperor and my country faithfully and I'm used to telling people the plain truth to their faces. I admit I have a quick temper, but really this is enough to make anyone explode.'

Gradually he cooled down sufficiently to tell her the details of my elder brother's arrival that morning and how he had lent his carriage so that Andrei and his younger brother could visit me, and so forth. 'Believe me, Madame,' he said, 'I have the utmost respect for you and my only complaint is that you have been too lax and indulgent. . . . It is obvious to me now that the whole thing is a result of your angelic kind-heartedness.'

As soon as the Principal could manage to interrupt the flow of my uncle's rhetoric she told him she considered that his anger was perfectly justifiable and that she could tell from the way he had taken his niece's interests so much to heart what a kind and noble person he really was. At these words my uncle, always susceptible to flattery, capitulated completely.

'There was no choice,' he said emphatically. 'My niece, my own sister's child, has no father, and I am her sole protector and benefactor. But you, Madame, as I have already told my niece a thousand times, are a wonderful woman, a true saint . . . but as for that Directress of yours——'

Here, however, the Principal was so scared that my uncle might say something that even the walls should not hear, that she hurriedly interrupted: 'I beg you, General, most generous and best of generals, give me your word of honour that this matter will never go further than this room!'

'I should be quite content to leave it at that', my uncle answered, 'so long as you undertake to make sure that Mlle Tufayev does not make the poor girl's life hell.'

'You can leave that to me!' the Principal assured him.

When I was led into her room Uncle got up from his chair and confronted me with a menacing shake of his two fingers; then he read me a lengthy lecture in a stern voice. 'Above all I expect from you a complete and unquestioning obedience to the authorities,' he said.

As we came out of the Principal's room I had a glimpse of a figure darting across the passage and guessed it was Masha Ratmanov trying to find out what had been happening. Everybody was already in bed by the time I reached the dormitory, but Masha jumped out from between her blankets fully dressed and began to ply me with questions; and all the others sat up in bed and eagerly begged me to tell them all the details in the proper order. However, I did not feel like talking and could only answer vaguely and unwillingly. This surprised my friends, who expected me to be feeling triumphant; but the fear that had nagged me all day, and the realization that only luck had got me out of trouble, had played on my jagged nerves so much that I could only throw myself on to my bed and, hiding my head in the pillow, burst into bitter tears.

The next day the Principal went to see the Directress. Their conversation remained a mystery, and we never learned either what the Principal said in the course of a lengthy interview she had with Mlle Tufayev; but for several days afterwards Mlle Tufayev's expression was bitter and defeated. She sat quietly in the classroom without lifting her eyes from the inevitable stocking and did not reprimand us even when we began to be noisy and ill-behaved. Me she left completely alone, not even mentioning my name.

As far as the Principal was concerned I was treated from then on with very special care and even invited to her room in our free period after dinner. On these evenings she made me read aloud from a French translation of Walter Scott, explaining anything I could not understand, and often she inquired about my family.

8

The New Inspector

One day when I got back to the dormitory after seeing the Principal, Masha Ratmanov came up with a sneer and said: 'You call yourself a desperado but you're pretty cunning about it—managing to be the Principal's favourite at the same time!'

I stared at her in astonishment. 'Maman may be in authority but she's a wonderful woman, a real saint,' I said eventually. 'I don't see that there's anything wrong in going to see her. She's not the type to try and find out what is going on in the classroom; I'm sure I haven't done anyone any harm.'

'Nobody says you have,' answered another girl. 'Not everybody agrees that she's a saint, though. . . . I expect everybody would go and see her if they were asked, but it's hardly the thing to do.'

This embarrassed me even more than Masha's accusation. 'But why, why?' I mumbled.

'Because the bigger distance we keep from the staff the better.'

'Wonderful woman, saint,' Masha repeated scornfully. 'Here we all are starving and your "wonderful woman" can't say a word to the bursar to stop us being deprived of our food. When a mistress complains about us, Maman always takes her side rather than ours. And it wasn't so long ago she advised you to go on your knees before Mlle Tufayev when she knew perfectly well the woman had lied about you.'

I stood stunned by this new notion, but at that moment a girl ran in from the corridor shouting: 'Why aren't you coming into the dining-room? The bell went ages ago.' We hurried to form pairs and go downstairs. I ran mechanically after the others without looking where I went, thinking over what the girls had said. 'They're right, perfectly right,' I told myself. 'What has Maman ever done to help us? The only difference between her and the others is that she is never actually rude to us, and here I am delighted at the thought of her being a saint.'

Suddenly I tripped and fell down the stairs; at one of the turnings I almost managed to save myself but the girls running past pushed into me and down I rolled again, falling the length of the stairs and crashing into the dining-room door. When my friends lifted me up I was conscious of nothing but a mass of red dots swimming before my eyes. I stood up for a moment and then, not feeling any pain, went with the others into the dining-room. Soon I felt perfectly all right and when we returned to the dormitory I went to bed and fell asleep with the others.

I woke up in the night with a pain in the chest and feeling feverish, but I covered myself with my coat and went to sleep again; but when the bell went in the morning I felt I could not lift my head from the pillow. Eventually I managed to raise myself but my head swam so much and my arms and legs trembled so much from weakness that I fell back on to the bed.

My friends helped me to get up. 'Whatever's the matter with you? You're covered with bruises, black and blue all over, your chest and neck are all swollen up,' they exclaimed in turn. After a discussion they unanimously decided I could not be sent to the sickroom, which would entail uncovering my chest to the doctor and thus disgracing not only myself but the entire form. I naturally shared this view and decided there was nothing else for it but to overcome the weakness and pain, get up, and go to the classroom as though nothing was wrong.

When we went to the classroom after breakfast they decided after consultation to ask the form-mistress whether I might keep my cape on during lessons: normally the rule at Smolny was that they had to be taken off. 'She has a cough,' they explained, 'but she does not want to go to the sickroom and miss her lessons for such a trifle.'

The request was granted but the linen cape was no protection from the cold and I shook all over from the rising fever. The girls then collected a lot of scarves which they wrapped round my feet and hands, telling me to keep them under my desk.

I sat and walked like an automaton. Sometimes I could not repress a groan, and the girls stamped their feet and coughed and begged me not to do it again. At dinner I could not eat a thing and my portion was speedily divided.

Next morning after a sleepless night I could scarcely get up; the swelling on my neck and chest was even worse. My friends decided that this was because I did not eat, and at breakfast and lunch made me force something down. When we got back to the classroom after dinner, however, I felt so sick that they hardly had time to drag me to the basin in the corridor, where traces of vomiting could be concealed, and then pour cold water over my head which felt as though it were on fire.

Throughout the next night the girls hurried to my bedside in relays to make sure I was covered up and to change the wet towel on my head, but I felt worse and worse and on the third day was quite unable to get up.

'Her chest's quite blue!' exclaimed one. 'And her neck is

more swollen than ever,' said another. 'But she must get up,' they decided, and began to dress me in bed, persuading me to be brave and carry on until the last possible moment.

When at last they got me on my feet they realized it would be impossible to lead me down the stairs and they decided to hide me, with one of the girls to look after me, just while the others were in the dining-room. We never had a roll-call and no set places were laid at breakfast, so the absence of one or two girls would never be noticed.

When they went to the classroom, which was on the same floor as our dormitory, my guards dragged me along and sat me on a bench. Trying hard not to fall off, and repressing my groans only with difficulty, I gazed at the girls with blank despair. Once again several of them asked the mistress if I could keep my cape on, but remembering the same request had been made the previous day she refused; thinking some kind of trick was being played on her she told me to come up to her.

My friends told me in frightened whispers what I ought to say about my bruises and swellings, but I was not listening. I summoned up enough strength to rise slowly and took a few tottering steps forward. The form-mistress and the blackboard and the orderly rows of desks suddenly swayed, the floor unexpectedly slid from under my feet and before I could say a single word I fell with a crash.

I recovered consciousness in a private ward of the sick-room which was usually kept for those who were seriously ill. Several people were there—the Principal, the sickroom matron and nurse, and three men of whom I recognized only the Institute's doctor.

One of the strangers, a man with a square-cut black beard, bent over me and asked my name.

'Elizabeth Tsevlovsky,' I answered, thinking how feeble and far-away my voice sounded.

'There is nothing wrong with her mind,' said the beard quietly, turning toward the Principal.

'Thank God,' whispered Maman as she dabbed a lace handkerchief on her eyes.

I looked round in astonishment until our doctor came forward, took my hand, and asked how long I had been in hospital.

'Two or three hours,' I said, surprised.

'You have been lying here eleven days, delirious all the time, and you have just been operated on,' he said. 'Try to eat and sleep as much as you can.'

I lay in hospital for two months without regaining enough strength to sit up in bed; the seriousness of my condition may be judged by the fact that although I had to submit to being bandaged twice a day the thought of my 'shame' never entered my head.

However, one day when I felt better the surgeon who had operated on me sat down by my bed and asked why I had not reported sick immediately after my fall down the stairs. At first I would not answer, but he was insistent.

'I just didn't,' I said at last.

'But I cannot believe you decided to put up with such suffering without a very good reason,' he objected.

I said nothing.

'I can see I shall have to answer for her,' the Institute doctor broke in. 'I know all their secrets. . . . No one has ever told me this for a fact but I am positive that she and her friends think there is something to be ashamed of in having to uncover their chests before a doctor. It must have been her dearest friends who persuaded her not to report sick.'

'Really, what a pernicious place this Institute is,' said the surgeon and, turning to me, he added: 'Do you realize, my dear girl, that your modesty nearly cost you your life?'

I blushed but still said nothing. When the doctor returned

to my bedside after seeing the surgeon out I told him furiously: 'Will you please tell that precious surgeon that, genius or not, he's still a fool if he doesn't realize that any decent girl in my place would have done exactly the same. And tell him I'm not his "dear girl". And you can warn him that I'm not going to put up with having my dressings changed any longer, the only reason I couldn't stop them being done before was because I was too ill to do anything about it.' And I would not change my mind in spite of the Principal's attempts to persuade me.

When I saw the surgeon and the doctor coming the next day I grabbed the bedclothes and pulled them up to my neck, but one held my hands and the other pulled the bedclothes down again and undid my nightdress until he could change my bandages. It was all done so quickly and deftly, and the dressing of the wound was so painful, that all my protests left me and after that I did not struggle any more.

I heard a rumour not long before my recovery that the Tsar was going to visit Smolny, and when the day actually came the authorities lost their heads completely. The old Directress abandoned her apartments and scurried about like a shadow from one end of the building to the other. I was kept well informed of what was happening by the sickroom maid and the nurse.

The dinner ordered from the kitchen that day was such that none of the pupils had ever seen anything like it even on holidays. From early morning the corridors resounded to the noise of sweeping and scurrying. Despite its perfect cleanliness everything in the sickroom was hurriedly wiped down and cleaned. Beautifully dressed and perfumed, the Principal appeared and warned me that the Tsar was likely to look in, and told me the proper way to greet him and how I should weigh up every word and answer his questions carefully. Then she and the doctor began to think up answers for all the questions he was likely to ask, and finally I was changed from head to foot and covered with a new quilt.

And then the Tsar Alexander II entered my room accompanied by various school authorities, the doctor and the entire sickroom staff. Tall and straight, he stopped a few paces from my bed.

In trembling tones I said my greeting in French, and he responded with a slight inclination of the head. There was a moment's silence and he asked: 'Are you still suffering much?'

'I am much better now, Your Majesty.' The answer came quite smartly, for the Principal had foreseen this question.

'What do the doctors consider she needs to restore her to health?' asked the Tsar, turning to the doctor.

'Fresh air, Your Majesty, would help to make her stronger.'

The Tsar spoke to me again. 'Have you any relatives in St. Petersburg, Mademoiselle?'

I answered that my uncle, General Govetsky, had his home in the town.

'You may go and stay with him when the doctors give their permission and return here to finish your education when you are quite recovered,' he said in a cold even voice with eyes directed on one point; and added in the same tone: 'And while you are here, perhaps you would like some delicacies?'

Maman had not foreseen this question and in some confusion I searched for an answer.

'Thank you from the bottom of my heart, Your Majesty,' I replied at last. 'Here in the hospital everybody is very kind to me.' I deliberately stressed the word 'here' in the hope that he would realize I was referring only to the hospital, but he took no notice.

'If you want anything special', he said, 'let your doctor know. You shall have anything that does not harm your

The New Inspector

health.' With these words he slowly turned and left.

When the rest of the doctor's department had been inspected he came jubilantly running in and began to say how gracious the Tsar had been to me, what a long conversation he had honoured me with, how generous he had proved . . . now I would be fed: chicken, wine, anything I wanted. 'And you certainly deserve it,' he said with a smile, 'after the nice way you spoke about us!'

'Of course,' he added with a slight wink, 'I realize you singled us out in order to have a little dig at someone else, but then nobody realized that apart from the Principal.'

The Principal came back to see me, too. Despite her usual kindly tone I realized that she was not particularly pleased with me: it was obvious that she was annoyed I had spoken only of the kindness of the sickroom staff.

I was sorry to leave the sickroom. During my illness I had time to forget the cold of the dormitories, the meagre dinners, the shouts of the mistresses; and the only consolation I had was the thought that I only had one more year to spend within the Institute's walls.

At the beginning of our year in the graduation form a rumour began to circulate that a new Inspector had been appointed. There was a special Inspector as well as the Directress and Principal, and it was his job to supervise the masters who taught us and find replacements for those who died or were ill for long periods: but we hardly ever saw him. He visited the classrooms two or three times a year and attended the examinations each spring, but that was the limit of his duties.

What used to happen when a new Inspector was appointed to the Institute—it was a very rare occurrence—was that he would be ceremoniously led into each classroom by the Principal and told in French: 'Monsieur, may I commend to you the pupils of Form So-and-so.' Turning to us, she would announce: 'Demoiselles, your new Inspector!' and we would rise politely, curtsy, and listen while he uttered a few pleasantries. During the lesson questions would be put only to the brightest pupils, and when it ended the Inspector would comment on how astonished he was at our thorough knowledge of the subject.

Our first meeting with the new Inspector, Konstantin Ushinsky, was quite different. One day just as we were starting for the classroom door at the end of a lesson a slim dark-haired man of medium height ran up; ignoring our curtsies he waved his hat about and shouted: 'You are supposed to learn the rules of good behaviour here, but you don't even know that it's wrong to spoil other people's property with scent and stuff. Not everyone can afford to put up with these vulgarities, for all you know I might be too poor to buy another hat! But of course, why should we worry about poverty, it is, *fi donc*, too degrading.' And with another flourish of his hat he hurried off.

We were rooted to the spot with astonishment. 'Is this our new Inspector?' we asked each other in tones of amazement. 'He's hardly been here five minutes and he starts shouting at us as if we were peasants at the market instead of educated young ladies.'

'It's not as if we did it,' someone pointed out. 'It must have been somebody in another form.'

'But suppose it was one of us, pouring scent on a hat isn't a crime; we've always done it, a decent man would be flattered by it. . . .'

'What bad manners, though! Not at all *comme il faut*. . . .'

'And fancy talking about poverty in that vulgar way. . . .'

We stood in the middle of the classroom and continued in this vein until the bell called us to our German lesson.

The new Inspector came walking in his quick nervous

strides behind the fat ponderous German master. He bowed, and without giving the master a chance to open his mouth asked a girl from the back of the classroom to come up to the desk. Putting an open textbook in front of her he asked her to translate.

'We haven't prepared as far as this,' the girl told him. Neither she nor a second girl nor a third called out by Ushinsky managed to make anything of the unprepared passage.

The embarrassed German grunted and fidgeted on his chair, and said by way of excuse that French was always given pride of place at the Institute and that even the pupils hated doing German. Unsatisfied with his explanation, Ushinsky told him that he ought to make us like it by reading to us and telling us something of the best work by Goethe and Schiller.

'My dear Inspector,' the German answered with a pitying smile, 'I assure you that the works of these wonderful writers would prove completely incomprehensible and uninteresting to them.' Ushinsky's impatient reply was that only an idiot could fail to be interested in the work of genius.

Another incident which made a profound impression on us took place during the German lesson. The duty-mistress, Mlle Tufayev, who was keeping an eye on the class, suddenly pushed back her chair with a clatter, stood up and moved over to a bench where she began tearing something out of one of the girls' hands. We were quite used to such scenes but as she moved her chair Ushinsky looked up quickly and stared at her disapprovingly as though unable to understand the distraction. When Mlle Tufayev started struggling with the girl he called out: 'Please stop all this noise. Who asked you to stay in the classroom? The master is perfectly capable of keeping order himself.' And he sat back and got on with his work as though nothing had happened.

A Russian Childhood

Mlle Tufayev went pale but said nothing—probably from sheer surprise. The lesson continued and, convinced after questioning a few more girls, of our total illiteracy, he shrugged his shoulders crossly, rose, bowed, and made for the door. At this point Mlle Tufayev, who had been sitting by the door, jumped up and began: 'Allow me to inform you, sir, that we are put on classroom duty at the express wish of the authorities, and we . . . and I . . . have the utmost respect for authority.'

She was hurrying on but Ushinsky interrupted her. 'If you must sit here for no good reason', he said calmly, 'you might at least keep quiet instead of distracting the pupils' attention by tearing the paper out of their hands.'

Mlle Tufayev trembled with annoyance and rage. 'I have served on the staff here for thirty-six years. . . . I am over sixty, and I have never been treated like this before,' she said. 'This will be reported to the proper quarters.'

'If that is what your duties are, please carry on by all means,' smiled Ushinsky, going out and shutting the door behind him. Mlle Tufayev sat down again but was too agitated to pick up her inevitable knitting. Suddenly she reddened, blew her nose, and left the classroom.

For the first time we were left alone with the master. Nobody said anything. Our German, momentarily deep in thought, roused himself and began calling out all our names in turn. Masha Ratmanov, taking advantage of the duty-mistress's absence, pressed her handkerchief to her face as though she had a nose-bleed and ran out—obviously on a reconnaissance.

When we returned to the classroom Mlle Tufayev fortunately went off to drown her sorrows in coffee and we gathered for another noisy discussion full of interruptions.

'He's terribly bad-tempered. . . . He simply has no manners. . . . He said quite unblushingly he couldn't afford another hat.'

A girl called Ivanovsky joined in. 'That's not true. Anyway, I think he's absolutely wonderful.'

'Was it you that put scent all over his hat?'

'Yes, it was, I couldn't help it. I was just going along the lower corridor this morning and I suddenly saw him. When I saw how handsome he was I was absolutely transfixed. . . . I let him go by and then I ran up to the clothes-hangers and put scent on his hat and in his coat-pockets. It was jolly lucky I had some with me, I used up a whole bottle.'

No one approved of this; the others felt Ushinsky did not deserve such attention.

'I'll bet he gets rid of the German now,' somebody suggested.

'Not likely, the Directress will throw him out first.'

'Really,' Masha Ratmanov interrupted, 'none of you seems to understand a thing. He could throw out a dozen directresses like ours if he felt like it. Ushinsky has such a personality, such power . . . it's really incredible.'

'Power?' somebody objected. 'Cheek would be more like it.'

'Can't you realize what courage it takes, what power a man must have to speak the truth in people's faces? The mistresses tell you how wrong it is and you repeat it although you despise them. What feeble creatures you are, just like a flock of sheep.'

There were furious objections to these crushing comments but we realized that Masha had some fresh information about the Inspector: so after a brief skirmish we begged her to tell us what she had discovered.

Any other time she would have seized the opportunity to put one over on us but she just couldn't resist passing on the news. When she left the classroom, she told us, she bumped into Ushinsky talking to the Principal in the corridor. She hid round the corner and heard the entire conversation. Ushinsky was describing his encounter with Mlle Tufayev; but, not knowing her name, described her as 'That wizened old woman, you know . . . she was boasting how great a respect she had for authority, how she'd been on the staff for thirty-six years, how long she'd lived: I was tempted to tell her that elephants live even longer, but that there's no point in a long life if it isn't a useful one. However, I should only have been wasting my time.'

Maman began in her usual diplomatic way to persuade him not to take such a stern view of the staff. 'Where can you find educated people?' she asked with a sigh. But Ushinsky told her it ought to be possible if one tried hard, and that one must beware of those who could only fawn on authority.

'Fawn on authority, what a wonderful way of putting it!' we echoed, surprised at what was for us a novel expression.

Masha went on: 'And then he added that a new way of recruiting mistresses must be found and that all the old rubbish must be cleared away.'

We murmured admiringly and besought her to go on.

'He said all the old rubbish had to be cleared away because all the present staff did was to dull the girls' intelligence and harden their hearts.'

'Dull their intelligence, harden their hearts,' we repeated. It was the first time such sentiments had ever been expressed inside the walls of the Institute and we savoured them eagerly trying to extract their implications.

'Then Maman began to explain why a mistress has to be present during lessons, and she said that the master is much too busy teaching to ensure that everyone pays attention. But Ushinsky told her that when there were new masters they would hold the pupils' attention so closely that they

would no longer be liable to distraction. Maman asked him
if he really believed he could create an ideal Institute, and he
said that even if not he thought he could make this stagnant
pool more healthy.'

'Good heavens, Masha!' we cried. 'Did he really say
"stagnant pool"? How rude, what an insult to the Institute,
Maman should have shut him up at once. Go on, though:
what did she say to that?'

'Not a thing. And he didn't stop there, either——'

But the bell went for tea and we had to form pairs and go
down to the dining-room.

A few days later Ushinsky visited a lesson given by the
Russian master; his name was Sobolevsky and he was as tall
and thin as a post, with sunken cheeks and low forehead like
a skeleton, and hair cut so short that it stuck up like a hedge-
hog's bristles. He spluttered so much when he read or talked
that the girls who sat in the front row tried to move somewhere else.

He divided his lessons into two parts: first came a page of
grammar which had to be repeated word for word. He never
gave us dictation, and we should probably have forgotten
how to write had he not given us Krylov's fables one after
the other to copy out and learn by heart. Reading the fables
occupied the second half of the lesson: he was never pleased
with his pupils and always demonstrated to each girl how to
recite. This involved a proper performance.

He always acted the part of the animals. For the fox he
bent double and, crossing his eyes (he had a squint to begin
with), he put on a thin voice, waving a rolled-up copybook
behind his back with one hand to represent the fox's brush.
For the elephant he raised himself on tiptoe and used three
copybooks rolled up and joined together for the trunk.
Simultaneously, depending on what animal he was represent-

ing, he would run about growling or stand still, waggle his shoulders or bare his teeth.

Ushinsky came into the classroom just as Sobolevsky was reciting 'The Elephant and the Pug'; noticing him, our Russian teacher gave full rein to his artistic abilities. When he reached the words 'and barked at him, and squealed and jumped up' he ran round the classroom spinning like a top, his voice sounding just like the squeal of a dog whose tail has been trodden on. Ushinsky looked at him in amazement without saying anything for a moment, then suddenly, in order to bring the exhibition to an end, said loudly: 'I shall give you a dictation.'

When he had done so he examined several copybooks, remarked that there were more mistakes in the words than letters, and left the classroom shaking his head. Meeting Sobolevsky in the lower corridor later, he told him: 'I'm sure you have often been congratulated on your expressive reading, but really you're making a spectacle of yourself. Such clowning is most undignified for a teacher.' Not realizing that these words were his sentence, he answered with a bow that he would await the Inspector's decision with trepidation.

Ushinsky turned away and began to look for his overshoes. Sobolevsky hastened over to the clothes-stand and had already bent down and picked them up for him when Ushinsky snatched them indignantly and said with irritation: 'A lackey on the dais? No, really, this is too much. I've made up my mind already.'

As usual the conversation was overheard by one of the desperadoes; it made an immediate impression on us. 'A lackey on the dais, a lackey on the dais,' we repeated one after the other. 'Goodness, what wonderful expressions he uses—I shall really have to make a little notebook for myself and jot them all down. . . .'

The New Inspector

Anticipating victory already, we waited impatiently for Ushinsky to visit the classroom for a lesson by Starov, who taught us literature. Starov was a kind, mild man full of enthusiasm and everybody liked him—and as a result learned by heart and copied very carefully the sheets he had compiled for us instead of textbooks. The works of all the most important authors were listed on these sheets in chronological order with such notes as 'uplifting', 'perfect', 'beautiful' appearing frequently in the commentary. As we had never read the books he was commenting on, the context of the notes was naturally often rather obscure. Although Starov introduced us to our authors only in excerpts from their works both we and his fellow members of the staff considered him the best teacher in the Institute.

He was the only one who conversed with us not only during lessons but before and after. Often when he met a crowd of girls waiting for him in the corridor he would bow gaily to them all and, noticing that one was frowning, would tenderly inquire: 'Why have the storm-clouds gathered?' or something in the same vein. He was always quoting poetry both in and out of class.

A girl might stop him and say: 'Oh, Monsieur Starov, I am in trouble'—and go on to tell him that she had been punished, and why, and by whom. Starov would rush to the mistress at once, clasp her hands, and with tears in his eyes beg her to forgive the culprit. 'You have such a good and kind and wonderful nature,' he would exclaim, 'how can a single angry feeling survive for a moment in your heart, the heart of such a noble being, the heart of a woman? It is impossible. To punish? To persecute? And whom—such a young and innocent creature. Can you bring yourself to punish youth for its errors, its impulses? To forgive, to forgive—that is the destiny of a woman. A woman who forgives is, I swear it, an angel from heaven. No, no, I shall not leave you until I have obtained your pardon. See, I am falling on my knees before you. . . .'

Flattered by such charming sentiments, such as she might never have heard in her life before, the mistress usually gave in. 'Really, Monsieur Starov, you *are* an unusual person! So kind-hearted! Very well: for *you*'—and she would emphasize the last word—'for *you* I shall forgive.'

When we were due for our first literature lesson after Ushinsky's appointment we came out into the corridor together to meet him and, all speaking at once, told about what the new Inspector had said and done.

'Of course,' Starov admitted sadly, 'Monsieur Sobolevsky's behaviour *is* a little undignified, but the Inspector need not have been quite so insulting about it.'

When we told him Ushinsky's reaction to having scent poured all over his hat he became really indignant. 'Good gracious, fancy interpreting the poetic impulse of a young creature in such a crassly materialistic way!'

There was a moment's silence and he added in regretful tones: 'Well, my dear young ladies, perhaps I too shall be forced to part with you.'

'No, never!' we chorused. 'If he doesn't appreciate you it'll just prove he's ignorant. You can count on us, we'll never let it happen.'

Starov looked happily at all of us and permitted himself an almost inaudible murmur of 'Delightful creatures!' before straightening up and adding in hollow tones: 'But how little you know of what is happening in the world outside!'

With a mysterious smile he went on: 'I find your ignorance charming; it is the most precious possession of the youthful heart!'

Our conversation was interrupted by the bell, and we rushed into the classroom. We had barely taken our seats when the Principal came in, followed by Ushinsky—

who, much to our surprise, greeted Starov pleasantly.

'Do you wish to examine the girls?' Starov asked.

'No, please carry on the lesson as usual.'

Starov called out the best pupil and examined her on her preparation in Pushkin; she answered beautifully.

'Very well memorized,' said Ushinsky suddenly. 'Now forget the elaborate textbook phrases and just tell us the story of Eugene Onegin.'

The girl hung her head and remained silent.

At this point Starov interposed that the class had no library and that he could not lend us his only copy as he often lectured on the same writer on the same day in different schools.

'No library? Then why teach literature? Have you never taken the matter up with the authorities?'

'It's the way things have always been done here. How the library is run is no concern of mine.'

'Girls—stand up whoever has read *Dead Souls*!'

Nobody moved.

'This is ridiculous!' the Inspector exclaimed, and he began to question each of us in turn. 'Have *you* read it? Or you? Perhaps you know something else of Gogol's. No? Has anybody read any Pushkin? Or Lermontov? Or Griboyedov? It's impossible. I just don't believe it. Here you are in the middle of a course in literature and yet nobody was interested enough to read a single work. I've never heard anything like it!'

Nobody said anything. Ushinsky, getting more and more worked up, alternated between us and Starov. 'What's this cupboard stuffed with?' It was full of notebooks, slates and other schoolroom equipment; there were two or three shelves devoted to textbooks, Bibles and works by Anna Zontag.

Ushinsky irritably read off the title of a textbook, shrugged his shoulders and stood in front of the cupboard silent for a moment before slamming it closed and returning to his place.

'Please carry on,' he said, in a flat tone as he mopped his brow.

'I scarcely think it will be possible,' said Starov, greatly offended, with some sarcasm: but he took out a volume of Pushkin and began to read a poem—'The Mob'. Gradually carried away by his favourite pastime of verse-reading, he raised his voice and, swaying to the metre, pronounced the last four lines with unmistakable emotion.

Erect, with blazing eyes and quivering voice, he made every syllable a condemnation of the materialists who were incapable of appreciating the poetic and the divine.

'Unfortunately the girls are not familiar with Pushkin's more important works,' commented Ushinsky: 'but please continue. No doubt you are about to explain the passage?'

'There is no need to explain. They understand it perfectly; their artistic sense is highly developed.'

'No, really?' said Ushinsky with a smile. 'Artistic sense, eh? And how do you suppose they developed it when they are completely unfamiliar with any literary work of art?' Then he called a girl forward and asked her to explain the poem in her own words; but in spite of having listened very attentively neither she, nor another nor another, could produce any answer.

At this point the Principal came to the rescue. Starov was a remarkable pedagogue, she told Ushinsky; we loved his subject and worked very hard at it, but at the moment were too shy to find any answer.

'Perhaps,' replied Ushinsky with a dubious smile. 'Suppose we try to converse on paper, then. Let one of the girls read the poem out loud twice, and then the others can put down its contents in writing.' And he went out into the corridor.

Our compositions proved no good at all. Some of us managed to string a lot of high-sounding phrases together,

others ascribed the poet's words to the mob or vice versa.
All of us had a great many spelling mistakes. Luckily the bell
prevented Ushinsky from reading all our efforts out loud and
he took them away with him.

We made up our minds that the new Inspector would take
pity on our favourite master if we all spoke out in his defence
—believing that if his pupils had a good opinion of their
master no one could possibly question it. Although we appreciated the difficulty of talking to Ushinsky, who made even
the staff feel embarrassed and confused, we were determined
to defend Starov to our last drop of blood. Shy as we might
be of people in general and Ushinsky in particular, however
bad at expressing ourselves, we would make any sacrifice for
the sake of our beloved master.

Having agreed in advance that one of us would mention
his wonderful kindness, another his teaching ability and a
third his fine poetic gifts we waylaid Ushinsky in the
corridor next day and ran up to him the moment he appeared.

'Monsieur l'Inspecteur, Monsieur l'Inspecteur,' we began.

'Please don't be so formal,' he answered; and his unexpected
offer took us aback so much that we even forgot what it was
we wanted to speak to him about.

'What is it you wanted to say? Please don't be shy, ask me
anything you like.' Noticing our scared expressions, he
added with a smile: 'Don't be cross with me for my brusque-
ness and the impolite way I sometimes talk. I have so much
work to get through that I do sometimes save time by drop-
ping the words which add a little polish to what one has to
say. Tell me, what's the trouble?'

We all nudged Masha Ratmanov, who was supposed to
speak first, but even she seemed slightly overcome and could
only mutter: 'You don't like Monsieur Starov, but really it
isn't his fault that we aren't given books to read.'

'You don't really know him,' said the girl supposed to detail his noble qualities. 'He's so kind. He's a simply wonderful man.'

'Yes, yes,' agreed Ushinsky. 'He's very kind and very nice, but unfortunately that isn't enough for a teacher.'

'Perhaps', said the girl timidly who had to praise his gifts, 'you don't realize he's a poet, a famous one too?'

'No, I'd no idea that there was such a poet. And a famous one, you say. . . . Tell me, what has he written? I expect he has familiarized you with his work at some length?'

Ushinsky's bantering tone reduced us to helplessness. We looked at each other and pushed the third girl forward again.

'There's a wonderful poem of his called "Prayer",' she whispered at last. Ushinsky persuaded her to recite it, and with a trembling voice she began:

> *Though as a child I hearkened oft*
> *To lamentations o'er the dead*
> *And, later, all their misery*
> *Would ponder in my youthful head,*
> *I, Starov, vowed I should not be*
> *Of gloomy thoughts the willing slave—*
> *But rather savour to the full*
> *The joy of living that He gave*
> *Who. . . .*

'That's enough, that's enough,' said Ushinsky with a wave of his hand. 'What it's all about heaven only knows. Starov has been lecturing on literature so long that he ought to realize by now that there is neither sense nor form nor feeling in his verses! And he is not ashamed to show all this Thoughts on Mortality rubbish to his pupils . . . really, it's complete nonsense whatever you may say; I assure you there's no need to grieve for *him*. As a matter of fact I have a much better master in mind for you.'

'What is his name?'

'Vodovosov.'

'What a funny name!' laughed somebody.

'You needn't laugh,' said Ushinsky severely. 'Among other things, he'll teach you what is funny and what isn't.'

One small thing happened which showed us that Ushinsky was a friend to us as well as an authority. Mlle Tufayev gave Anya Ivanovsky a letter from her father one day; and forthwith began to reproach her in front of the whole class for giving herself airs when her father had nothing, and preferred to spend what money came his way on going to the theatre instead of sending any to his daughter. Anya blushed and tears came to her eyes as she took the letter and ran out into the corridor. It was true that her father said in his letter that he could not let her have any money this time because his affairs were in a poor state. She put the letter in her apron pocket and waited for some time in the corridor because she did not wish to go back to the classroom with her eyes still red.

Suddenly Ushinsky came along. He persuaded her to tell him why she was looking so unhappy, and she explained how the girls could only correspond with their parents through the form-mistresses. That was the rule and there was nothing she could do about it, but all the same she was angry with herself for not doing the same as all the other girls— that is, entrust their letters to a relative and arrange to receive a reply in the same way. Anya told him quite honestly that she was not upset about having been refused the money, but by the treatment of Mlle Tufayev who had made use of her father's letter to read her a lecture and insult her in front of everyone else.

Ushinsky thanked her warmly for confiding in him and said he would do all he could to bring the custom to an end;

and indeed not long afterwards the form-mistresses began passing on the girls' letters without opening them.

Another custom he succeeded in getting rid of was removing our capes during lessons. 'Perhaps you will be against the girls appearing at our balls with bare shoulders,' suggested the Principal with a sarcastic smile.

'I assure you I have no intention of interfering with their appearance on such occasions,' he answered lightly; 'but look at it this way: girls go to dances in order to attract husbands. The classrooms, however, are dedicated to learning; and yet shoulders are bared, presumably for the benefit of the master. I know from my own observations that they put their capes on again when the lesson is over.'

Ushinsky also got rid of another more pernicious tradition. Before his arrival we were not allowed to ask the masters questions during lessons. He insisted we should ask about anything we could not understand, and in fact achieved the result of turning lessons into lively discussions between master and pupils.

9

New Ideas and Old

One day, when there were only a few months left before the end of our final year at Smolny, Ushinsky came up to me and asked: 'Was it you who made such a martyr of yourself when you fell down the stairs, and nearly died rather than go to the doctor and disgrace yourself?'

I did not answer because I thought there was scorn in his inquiry, but my friends told him he was right; whereupon our stern Inspector, who smiled so rarely, burst out laughing. I blushed. Thinking he was making fun of me I turned to go without even curtsying, which was considered the height of rudeness.

'Why are you so cross?' asked Ushinsky in amazement as he stopped me: 'Have I offended you?'

'Any girl in my place would have done the same thing,' I answered flatly.

'Come now,' he said good-naturedly, 'even if you all felt exactly the same way (and this time there was no trace of mockery in his voice) very few would have managed to keep it up right to the end. Really you were a heroine! Such will-power and character should be put to some use. . . . What I am suggesting is, briefly, that instead of going home at the end of the year you should stay on and join the new seventh-year class I am organizing. The idea is that you should read, think, use your intelligence until even the matter we were discussing just now will appear to you in a different light.'

I was so surprised by his sudden suggestion that I could find nothing to say. When he saw my hesitation Ushinsky said that he did not want to hurry me; if I liked the idea I would have to ask my parents' permission, but there was plenty of time yet.

For the first occasion during my entire life at Smolny I wrote to my mother what was not an 'official' letter. I wrote about the new Inspector who had appeared on the scene and his ideas and reforms, about the new class in which new masters were going to teach; I told her Ushinsky had suggested I should stay on for it, and asked her permission to do so.

All Ushinsky's reforms were due to come into force at the beginning of the following year. Girls were to stay at Smolny seven years instead of six, and the curriculum was to be not only altered but considerably widened. New subjects to be introduced included natural history and physics, which were to be taught with the aid of models, stuffed animals, charts, experiments and various forms of apparatus.

Even here he might have failed had he had not been helped by a piece of luck. During his thorough examination of every corner of the Institute he had discovered a door which was permanently locked. This interested him and he made inquiries about it, but neither the Directress nor the Principal could remember what lay behind it.

Ushinsky promptly called in a locksmith and had the mysterious door opened. He was confronted by a vast room with cases round the walls containing an extensive collection of stuffed animals, a beautiful herbarium and some expensive scientific equipment.

Astonished by his good fortune, the Inspector made further inquiries. It turned out that the treasures had been presented to Smolny by the two Tsarinas, Maria Fyodorovna and Alexandra Fyodorovna. Since these were imperial gifts the authorities had felt it incumbent upon them to guard them with great care, to the extent apparently of keeping them locked up in a separate room. Having hidden them so successfully the authorities must have forgotten their existence and seemed no less astonished than Ushinsky at the discovery.

The opening up of the museum was very exciting, and we kept running to have a look at it. Ushinsky found someone to take out the moth-eaten animals one by one and restore them; then the room was placed out of bounds, which of course made getting inside even more fascinating. One day another girl and I found Ushinsky had just left the museum, so we went in and started excitedly examining the stuffed animals which were standing about on the floor. We found a small furry animal; one of us maintained it was a sable, the other said a marten. Suddenly a young man emerged from behind a cupboard door and said: 'Actually, mesdemoiselles, it is neither. It is only a weasel. . . . Somebody told me that the pupils here couldn't tell the difference between a horse and a cow: is it true?'

'Certainly not!' I exclaimed indignantly.

'What a nasty thing to say,' commented the other girl. 'We'll tell Monsieur Ushinsky what you said.'

'Don't you even realize', was the answer, 'that it's wrong to tell tales?'

Shortly before the final examinations I heard from Mother again. 'Until now', she wrote, 'I have always been sorry that your letters were so dry and wooden. The change that has come over you, whom I had begun to think quite devoid of feeling, can only be due to a teacher who is a genius.' She went on to ask if I would convey Ushinsky not only her great respect but also her astonishment that he had been able to instil into such a lazy girl as me a desire to study. She was, in fact, happy to hear that I should be staying on at the Institute.

Leaving-day came; the chapel overflowed with people. Those of my friends who decided against staying on were about to be given their freedom; overcome with excitement in their fluffy white dresses, white belts and white gloves, some even had tears in their eyes and the very palest girls were flushed. Still in my old uniform I stood by the wall with a very heavy heart. 'Lucky things,' I was thinking, 'no being roused at dawn by that wretched bell for them to-morrow! Instead of the mistresses' shrieking and cursing all they will hear is the gentle voices of their families. Why, oh why, did I stay on? Nothing will come of my studying and none of it will be any use!'

I looked around among the gaily-dressed congregation and suddenly caught sight of Ushinsky and was almost overcome with anger at him for having persuaded me against leaving. Rather than burst out crying I left the chapel—and for the first time in my life nobody took any notice.

Running into an empty classroom I dropped my head on to a desk and gave way to utter despair—only to hear Ushinsky's quick tread behind me. It was too late to run away, and I felt that if he so much as spoke to me I would come straight out with everything: but when he asked what I was doing sitting there I was afraid my voice would betray my tears and I said nothing.

'Why are you always so shy?' he asked, pulling up a chair and putting his case on my desk. 'I suppose you're feeling miserable because you didn't put on a white frock and a white belt today like the rest of your friends? Do tell me, don't be so bashful.'

'What is there to be bashful about?' I began crossly. 'Anyhow, you're always laughing at us. . . .'

New Ideas and Old

'If you think that, you're sadly mistaken,' Ushinsky interrupted. 'If I sometimes smile as I listen to you, please believe me there is no malice in it. No decent man would want to laugh at you; after all, it's scarcely your fault that nobody taught you anything here and that you'd got hold of some pretty fantastic ideas.' And he asked again why I had left the chapel and what I was doing sitting there.

'I wasn't doing anything,' I retorted abruptly.

Ushinsky shook his head. 'How can anybody sit and do nothing? People who are serious about their work must be able to account for every minute.'

This made me feel a 'desperado' all over again. Without bothering about the impression I might be making on him I started to tell him everything that was going on in my head. 'I wasn't feeling just "miserable",' I said, 'I was completely overcome with despair. And it wasn't because I couldn't put on a white frock, it was because I agreed to stay on at the Institute and go on with the work I hate so much. I don't *want* to be educated, I don't *want* everybody to call me a blue-stocking.'

'There's no need to explode in the effort to show me how silly you can be,' Ushinsky broke in. 'Tell me, are you deliberately trying to say what you know will hurt me? After all, it's you who'll benefit if you do stay on at the Institute until you are not so silly. But if you've really decided not to go on working it would be better to ask your mother to take you away tomorrow.'

'I'm the unhappiest person in the whole world,' I sobbed, quite unashamed of the tears which by now were rolling down my face. 'My own mother instead of longing to see me again after all these years is delighted to hear that I am staying on. . . .'

'You've no right at all to speak about your mother like that,' said Ushinsky sternly. 'It's really very wicked of you.

I had a letter from her myself only the other day and I think she's an exceptionally intelligent woman; instead of writing a lot of sentimental twaddle she expressed the one hope that her daughter would go on working until she can call herself an educated woman.'

At this my anger suddenly evaporated; it was nice to hear Ushinsky defending my mother. But what else had she written to him?

'Tell me,' I said with some hesitation, 'when you read my mother's letter didn't you think she might be sucking up to you?'

Ushinsky roared with laughter. 'Oh dear, now you'll think I'm making fun of you again. But how can I possibly remain serious when you use such ridiculous expressions? I can assure you I did *not* think your mother was "sucking up" to me.' And he added with a smile: 'It looks as though I have a better opinion of her than her own daughter has.'

Noticing that my agitation had subsided, he changed the subject: 'It seems as though the storm has passed and we can talk business,' he said. 'Well, you've decided to stay here in spite of your despair: start reading, then. I've brought a book by Belinsky for you and several volumes of Pushkin. Have a little confidence in me: read *Eugene Onegin* first and then Belinsky's article on it immediately afterwards. Then read the rest of Pushkin in the same way. I should also like you to write down anything that enters your head on the subject. If you conscientiously do what I ask, I give you my word your vexation will disappear.'

I blushed silently, ashamed of all I had blurted out to Ushinsky.

Eventually the time came to begin our lessons and we awaited Ushinsky's first lecture with impatience. 'You should and must kindle in your hearts a perpetual desire for knowledge,' he said, and his words made a deep impression on us.

New Ideas and Old

Everything he said was new and the future which had seemed so obscure to us suddenly appeared in a fresh light. This very first lecture he gave made it impossible for us ever to return to the Institute's old ways of thinking; and not very long afterwards the new teachers began their work with us.

Their lectures were entirely different from what we had been used to. We were not only allowed to give our opinions but the masters actually tried to teach us how to express ourselves. During a lesson we were free to move about and ask questions; everything we said, however amusing or naïve it might sound to the master, was listened to with patience and readiness.

One day Ushinsky, who often visited the classrooms, came in during a geography lesson. When the bell rang we surrounded him and the master, and—as usual—began to talk to them without paying any attention to the duty-mistress; which naturally she did not like.

'I always knew you would make good progress under the new system,' Ushinsky said with some feeling, 'but you have surpassed my wildest expectations. And I do realize what an effort it must have been, considering you are not used to such concentrated work.'

Praise from our beloved Inspector was the best reward we could have asked for. There was nothing of the old business of 'adoration' in our feeling for Ushinsky; instead we felt for the staff a deep respect combined with grateful affection. We often talked to them nowadays, though previously such conversation had been forbidden. Some of the masters even came into the garden to talk to us and tell us about people they had met, plays they had seen, or books and articles they had read. One day a happy crowd of us was strolling in the garden with the master who took us for Russian Literature; we were using his name and patronymic, which would have been unheard of before, and he was addressing us in the same manner. At this moment two mistresses going in the opposite direction passed us.

'Good heavens, they are using Christian names,' cried Mlle Loparev, snatching her companion's hand in horror. 'Surely I must be mistaken!'

'You are quite right, my dear,' answered Mlle Tufayev. 'You are quite right. It wouldn't surprise me in the least if the next thing that happened was that they all played skipping games with that crazy Inspector.'

It was 1861. When the news of the liberation of the serfs was announced in the Institute a special service was held in the chapel, and a few hours later Ushinsky announced that he wished to explain the meaning of the manifesto.

Afraid to miss a single word, I listened to him attentively. I remembered walking with Nanny through the village and the wretched overcrowded huts of our peasants. I remembered their complaints, but it was only now that for the first time I really understood them. I remembered the bailiff Karla who tyrannized the serfs of my noble uncle—of whom I had felt so proud at the Institute. I remembered Makrina's behaviour and the pride of the impoverished nobility—the smallholders who despised work and were ashamed of poverty; and I remembered the screams and groans I had heard on the Voinovs' estate when at their master's orders the serfs were thrashed.

Not long after Ushinsky's speech he announced that a weekly class for the Institute's maids was to be held, and that seventh-year pupils who wished to teach them could give them lessons on Sundays. We all readily volunteered, and one Sunday after a service they had all attended we began classes for them. Ushinsky walked among us listening to our efforts at teaching and afterwards pointed out our mistakes to us.

New Ideas and Old

The new school for maids did not, however, last for very long: in its sudden and unexplained closure we might have recognized, had we been more experienced, the first indication of the storm which was gathering round Ushinsky. It seemed that somewhere beyond the walls of the Institute a strong wind was blowing up quite different from the one which was bringing us our breath of fresh air.

The authorities felt that the moment had come for them to open their campaign against him. On several occasions things were made unpleasant for him. The Directress became bolder, and in conversation with Ushinsky hinted that he had deliberately appointed new masters to spread wicked and dangerous ideas; she reproached him for undermining the moral foundations of the Institute and trying to dispense with feminine modesty and other Smolny virtues as though they were so much rubbish. Sensing her disapproval the mistresses became more subservient to her than ever and started spying on Ushinsky and the other masters. After classes they would now carry on animated conversation in whispers, or sit together at the side of the room talking loud enough for us to hear.

'That impudent wretch had the effrontery not to bow to me today,' one would announce. The other might answer that 'that creature' had looked at her in a most brazen fashion the day before, or had laughed right in Mlle Loparev's face, or had accidentally pushed into Mlle Tufayev without so much as apologizing. The name of the criminal was never mentioned but we gussed they were speaking of one of the young masters.

Counting on the Directress's sympathy and aware that the right moment had arrived, the mistresses began persecuting the girls at every step—calculating that by interfering with our studies they could annoy the masters and pay Ushinsky back a little. They took to getting up in the middle of lessons and marching up and down between the desks, so that if one of us happened to move a textbook or an exercise book she would scold her loudly, tidy up the desk and pull at the girl's cape as though straightening it.

Ushinsky was, however, not the type to let himself be pushed out without a struggle, and so the Directress simply decided to make his existence intolerable. With this idea she called in the Principal and instructed her to do everything she could to oppose all Ushinsky's reforms. She took the opportunity to announce that, although we might ask questions during a lesson, we must confine our inquiries to difficulties in that particular subject. In her opinion we were abusing the privilege by screaming and shouting round the masters between every lesson and talking a lot of nonsense. She was not prepared to put up with it any longer, nor could she allow the masters to enter the garden and talk with us.

So at one stroke our friendly relations with the masters came to an end, and—the severest possible punishment for us —complete silence reigned in the classrooms. We went on working and reading as hard as ever—but new questions were occurring to us all the time, and now there was no one to answer them.

One day when Mlle Tufayev was on duty, 'Maman' came into the classroom where we were waiting for Semevsky, who took us for Russian history. We rose from our places with the customary greeting and, speaking as usual in French, she told us in trembling tones: 'The ill-mannered youngster who is due to arrive here at any moment (Semevsky was the youngest of the masters) displays such a lack of elementary courtesy to everyone that I consider it my duty to teach him a lesson. I shall now leave the classroom and return when he arrives, whereupon I shall expect you all to leave your places quietly and follow Mlle Tufayev and myself out of the room. When he finds himself alone perhaps he may come to his senses.'

New Ideas and Old

The Principal had barely finished giving us these strange orders when the bell for the next lesson rang and she hurriedly left. The master arrived and made the usual bow to Mlle Tufayev, but met with no response. We rose to greet him but at that moment the Principal reappeared; we remained standing and the master, who had already sat down, rose again and bowed to her: but she raised her head still higher and grandly swept out.

However, everything did not go according to plan. Mlle Tufayev went out and the girls followed her in an embarrassed manner—but not all of them; Masha Ratmanov, Anya Ivanovsky and I stayed in our places. The master, still on his feet, looked round with a bewildered expression: none of us made a sound. Eventually he sat down and began to take his books out of his case. Then, as though in apology to the three of us, he said: 'In the circumstances I can hardly give my lecture,' bowed, and left the room.

His departure was a signal for the others to return. First came the Principal, tears running down her cheeks: she turned to us who had stayed behind and asked in tones vibrant with anger and indignation: 'How dare you disobey me, you three? I have never been so insulted before, and this is how you treat me after I have lavished nothing but kindness and affection on you!'

Anya burst into tears and ran up to her. 'Forgive me, Maman, I did not think. I never realized you would be so upset, Maman. You're the nicest person there is here.'

The Principal did not answer but put a handkerchief to her eyes and went off to her own apartments; Anya ran after her begging her not to be cross, and was very soon forgiven.

In the evening she sent for me and repeated everything she said in the classroom. Again I made no response and she suddenly asked: 'Is there some grudge you have against me? I have no hesitation, since I have never done you or any of the others any harm, in asking. In fact I have always defended all of you—and you in particular—before the mistresses.'

'Of course I have no grudge against you, Maman. There is no reason why I should have. I assure you that I am very sorry I hurt you.'

'In that case you should have come to me and begged my pardon today.'

'I could not, it would have been against my principles.'

'Against your what?' she asked scornfully, and smiled sarcastically without waiting for me to reply. 'So that's the kind of thing the new masters have taught you, a lot of high-flown phrases?'

'Repeating a lot of meaningless words may be using high-flown phrases, but I know what a principle is and I am quite ready to suffer for it,' I said firmly.

'You must be mad, I've never had such a thing said to me before. Your judgement has been completely warped by the new masters.'

'Probably nobody has said anything like this before because both principles and opinions were unknown.'

'If your drawing-room conversation is like this you will be a complete laughing-stock'; and she laughed nervously before calming down and continuing in serious tones: 'Perhaps you would be good enough to explain the connection between your high principles and my orders.'

Pausing for thought over every word, I answered slowly: 'Maman, you told us to leave the classroom in order to punish the master for his discourtesy. But in front of us all the masters always bow to the mistresses, even though nowadays they are always ignored. Their behaviour to us is always scrupulously correct and they take a deep concern over our education. Why should we punish them? It would have been a very mean thing to do on our part, and that is why your instructions were against my principles.'

New Ideas and Old

'You wretched girl, your whole nature's been completely twisted! Leave the room immediately!' she shouted—adding, when I curtsied before going: 'You'll be expelled, I shall insist upon it—you before Masha Ratmanov! Your presence here is nothing but a menace to your friends. There is nothing your uncle can do to save you this time.'

Although I had been longing for Maman to finish the conversation so that I could run back to my room, I now felt I could not leave until I had expressed everything prompted by my anger and indignation.

'You needn't worry about being bothered by my uncle,' I began impertinently. 'Eighteen months ago I may have knelt before you and kissed your hands and begged you to protect me from slander——'

'But I suppose now with all your high-faluting principles such a thing would be too humiliating for you,' she interrupted.

'It isn't that. If I had been expelled from the Institute then I should not have known what to do with myself, but things are quite different now. I'm so determined to study and earn my own living that nothing on earth is going to stop me. You say that my drawing-room conversation will get me laughed at, but I'm not going into your precious drawing-rooms—all I want to do is study. It was the new masters here who made me feel this way, but all you want me to do is make things difficult for them.'

'And why do you and Masha consider yourselves so vastly superior to the other girls who lacked the effrontery to disobey me?'

'We don't at all. It's merely that they were taken unawares and had no time to think things over. Usually I do what the others do, that's the way we've been trained here. . . .'

This absolutely infuriated the Principal. 'The best way of stopping your quick thinking is to have you thrown out of here,' she cried.

'I'll tell my family. . . .'

'No you won't, they'll hear officially from the Institute. And now kindly remove that apron and leave it off until the day you are expelled. Don't wear it in chapel, either, and stay away from the others.'

'You can expel me if you want to, but I won't be punished as if I were a child. I'm grown up, and I won't do it.' My voice rose to a shout as I dropped a quick curtsy and left the room.

'Get out of my sight!' I heard her shout behind me.

This time I was sure I was going to be expelled; it was not Mlle Tufayev but the Principal herself, who rarely used such threats, who had said so. I left her room with burning cheeks and a hammering heart.

In the corridor I met some girls and asked them to tell the duty-mistress that I felt unwell and had gone to the sickroom: it was the only way I could calm down and think over my situation. As I lay in bed in the sickroom that night I went over all that had happened in my mind trying to find a way out. I decided there was only one thing I could do—let Ushinsky know.

I spent all that night thinking over a letter to him and the next day I started to write it. I told him how the Principal had instructed us to walk out of the classroom, explained why I had felt unable to do it, and reported my conversation with Maman. I had no doubt I should be expelled, I wrote, and asked if he would continue to superintend my studies after I had left the Institute.

Two days later Masha Ratmanov came to see me. The Principal had of course gone to see the Directress, she told me, in spite of which nothing had been done about us.

When over a week went by and still nothing happened I decided to return to the classroom. Ushinsky, I learned, had been away all that time.

New Ideas and Old

On his return he spent a long time with the Principal: we never heard what they talked about, but somehow Masha and I felt reassured and indeed from then on nobody bothered us—a fact for which we realized we had Ushinsky to thank.

Time was flying now, and we were all working feverishly during the few days left to us before our departure from the Institute. Shortly before my final examinations Mother arrived in St. Petersburg; our meeting affected me far more than I would ever have thought possible. She had altered a great deal during our separation—she was much stouter, and there was a network of wrinkles over her face I had not seen before. Her faded eyes seemed softer and kinder, and the restless energy was missing from her movements. Her old-fashioned black frock and simple practical way of talking reminded me of something dear and long forgotten; for a long time I held her in my arms and I felt that the old unspoken animosity between us had vanished and we could be friends at last.

The month which followed the final examinations was devoted to preparations for the official school-leaving day. Inwardly I still seethed with anger against the Institute and its regime; and the idea of smiling my way through the celebrations had no appeal for me. I tried to find a way of escaping the festivities by leaving the Institute as soon as the examinations were over, and eventually I hit on a plan which seemed to have a good chance of being accepted by the authorities.

The night before the examinations ended I went to see the Principal—our first encounter since that last unfortunate interview. In short businesslike sentences I explained that my mother had come a long way to St. Petersburg and, although she was staying with my uncle, found it inconvenient to stay away from home for so long; could I have permission, I asked, to leave the Institute without waiting for the official day.

'If you wish,' Maman replied with an expression of surprise and in tones which suggested she did not believe my explanation.

The examinations ended at noon the next day. When my friends went in to lunch I ran trembling with excitement to the dormitory; I had to let Mother know I was free and could leave the Institute the next day. Throwing on my hat and coat I ran downstairs and out into the garden. For the first time I had to venture into the streets alone. Taking care no one should notice me, I made my way to the gates. Luck was with me and the porter, busy talking to one of the maids, did not see me as I slipped past.

It was a clear frosty day: the road stretched before me, and a few paces from me was a sleigh. What lovely weather for a drive! 'So this is freedom,' I thought with renewed delight at having decided to leave the Institute early. Jumping into the sleigh I gave the driver my uncle's address and told him to drive fast.

As we went over a bridge I watched with incredulous eyes the spectacle of people below me crossing the Neva on foot. 'How can the ice hold them?' I wondered. 'Why don't they fall through into the water?' Everything seemed so strange. Other sleighs came rushing towards us and each time one drew level I cried out and put my hands over my face: but by some miracle we were unscathed.

By the time we got to my uncle's I was completely unnerved and wished I had never embarked on the terrifying journey across the town. 'Here you are, Miss,' said the driver as he pulled up. I jumped down quickly on to the pavement and tore up the stairs towards the big doors in front of me, only to stop at the sound of a rough voice calling out behind me. 'The fare—what about my fare?' the driver shouted.

'Good heavens, he's demanding money, he must have decided to rob me in broad daylight,' I thought. 'He'll attack me at any minute.' And I rushed in and up the stairs as fast as I could, the driver pounding along behind me. I nearly fell and clutched at the banisters: what would have happened next, had not a door on the landing chanced to open and my aunt emerge, I cannot imagine. So scared I could hardly get my breath, I stammered out that the driver was trying to rob me: unable to catch a word I said she peered at me in short-sighted bewilderment. But then the driver came up to us and spoke to my aunt.

'It's like this, Ma'am,' he said. 'She got in just outside Smolny and never argued about the fare and I thought aha, a real young lady, might even give me a good tip. Right across the town we came, and then she ran off without paying. I can't let you get away with that, I thought, so I left the horse and came after her.'

At last my aunt realized what had happened. 'It's all right,' she said with a smile, 'I'll pay you: the young lady's only just come out of the Institute, and she didn't understand.'

'I thought there must be something,' said the driver as he accepted his fare. 'She's not right in the head, a bit touched, I thought: kept on screaming all the way as if she was scared of something.'

When my aunt took me in, all the family—including my mother—hurried to greet me and began showering me with questions. I was scolded for having come by myself and without permission: their chief concern was to get me back again as soon as possible. Uncle ordered the coach to be brought, and my mother hurriedly got ready to accompany me. When we returned together nobody asked where we had been: since my mother was with me everybody took it for granted I had been out in the garden with her. So it was that the crime I committed on my last day at Smolny went undetected.

The next day Mother came to my dormitory to fetch me:

my friends were laughing and chattering round me as they helped me to collect my things together and pack. Mother listened with amusement and when everything was ready I kissed my friends warmly and went with her to say good-bye to the Principal. As we came down the stairs the porter said that the Inspector had asked us to see him in the examination room.

The realization that I was saying farewell to him and would lose touch with him for ever was like a knife in my heart, and though I was doing my utmost not to cry the tears were pouring down my face.

Ushinsky put his hand on my shoulder. 'Ah, there you are,' he said with a slight smile. He was always embarrassed at the sight of tears.

'Well, well . . . I was in a hurry to get you here because I was afraid you might be rushing triumphantly about and making a nuisance of yourself again. Have you managed to yet?'

Choked by tears, I could only shake my head.

'Splendid. I needn't lecture you, then.' And, seeing I was still unable to control myself, he patted my shoulder and went on: 'I want you to know that I never intend to part with any of my pupils. Even if you go to the other end of the world you will have to let me know how your work is getting on: I must be brutal with you, you see.'

My mother smilingly commented that there was no need for force now that I was completely preoccupied with work.

'You don't always want to believe what she says,' Ushinsky replied in the same vein. 'She's an excitable young lady . . . though I admit that lately she's been working very hard indeed. Don't think I have anything against amusement, though: it's just that I believe work should come first and amusement afterwards.'

New Ideas and Old

As he gave me his hand in farewell, he suddenly asked: 'Have you said good-bye to everyone?'

I answered that I still had to appear before the Directress, who had sent word through the Principal that she wished to see me. Ushinsky looked at me with his steady gaze and said severely: 'I hope you will not disgrace yourself by doing anything silly.'

As soon as we were shown into her reception room, Mother and I went over to the table at which the Directress was sitting: with a bare nod of her head she began to speak at once. Addressing herself to my mother, and articulating each syllable as distinctly as though she wished to hammer it into her head, she announced that the Institute authorities were delighted at being relieved of my presence so soon.

Mother listened with a frown, and I began to hope that everything would be all right when suddenly the Directress began to recall what she called 'the unsavoury incident involving your sons, in which the General played such an undignified role and made things so difficult for all concerned'.

At this point Mother could keep her quick temper no longer. Looking the Directress straight in the eye, she declared that only the Institute authorities could have made anything unseemly out of two brothers visiting their sister: and as far as her brother the General was concerned, she ought to be grateful that he had not let the Tsar hear all about what had happened. Mother added that she could not understand why the Directress had found it necessary to bring up an incident which was entirely due to the Institute authorities having taken at their face value the slanderous allegations of one of the mistresses. She said frankly that she thought the Directress had raised the matter because she was so used to speaking to her subordinates, who never dared to contradict her: but as far as she was concerned she saw no reason to listen in silence to the repetition of what even the Institute authorities now recognized as slander.

While Mother was speaking the Directress's face changed colour several times: eventually she rose majestically from her seat and pointed angrily to the door, a gesture which Mother ignored until she had finished what she had to say. We were already half-way down the stairs when the Directress's companion caught us up and held out a book to me, muttering in horrified tones: 'I don't know how you dared be so rude to the Directress. Even so, Her Excellency is so angelically kind, so infinitely forgiving that she told me to give you this Bible just the same. She says she hopes the Good Book——'

But realizing that Mother, who was still seething, was on the point of making some answer, I snatched the book and dragged Mother downstairs after me.

My heart beat rapidly as we drew near Pogoreloye again: here was the familiar hill, there at the foot of it our lake. And there in the distance was a glimpse of the roof of the house.

Mother had told the entire family of our arrival and asked them all to be there so that we could all spend a few days together under our own roof. Our first moments of meeting were quite incoherent. Questions were fired at me from all sides and I answered them anyhow; I asked questions myself and in my eagerness to embrace them all in turn often did not wait for the answers. Tears were blinding me so that I could not even see my brothers' and sisters' faces properly.

At last dinner was announced and we went to the table, each of us from force of habit taking his old place. And now I had a chance to take a proper look at them all.

Heavens, how Nyuta had changed . . . how old and ugly she had become. Her face was flabby and wrinkles—made by tears, perhaps?—radiated from her eyes. *Old and ugly*, I thought: and remembered how, only a few years previously, she had been renowned as a beauty.

And how Sasha had altered, too. I was amazed when I looked at my favourite sister. Her eyes were sad, her face had lost its lively mobility, and there was a deep furrow on her brow.

Only my brothers, Andrei in particular, looked well. Well built and handsome, he looked wonderful in his new officer's uniform, and Mother could not take her eyes off her favourite for the whole of dinner.

Between the courses I asked Mother if I might leave the table and look at the rooms I had not yet seen. Everything was exactly as it had been during my childhood.

Then, suddenly, I found myself standing stock-still in the middle of the ballroom. It was as though somebody had lifted a curtain before my eyes and I could see down to the last detail scenes from my miserable, lonely, neglected childhood. Memories overwhelmed me like a flood and I could see things as though they had happened only yesterday. Everything round me—furniture, walls, decorations—reminded me of the terrors of the past. There was the low table I had worked at, the one where Savelyev had tied me when he wanted to give me a good thrashing. And there was the arm-chair in which he sat when he used to make me report on what my sister had been doing. . . .

Upset by these memories I ran to the nursery. In the corner was the icon before which I had prayed God so passionately night after night to kill Savelyev and make my mother love me. Nanny's wooden bed, black with age, was still there. How often I had crawled into it at night when I was frightened. Sasha had slept there too—the two people who had tried to protect me during my wretched childhood.

Choking with tears, I fell on my knees before the bed that

was so dear to me. Then a sudden burst of laughter from the dining-room made me jump, and I got up and slipped through the adjoining room to cool my burning face on the porch.

Andrei came to fetch me in. 'What's the matter?' he asked, looking at me in some concern. He led me by the arm into the dining-room, saying with a smile: 'Here's the romantic creature who can even shed tears over a sparrow's grave.'

'Tell us, why the tears?' asked Mother tenderly. 'Don't you enjoy recalling your childhood?'

Her words cut me to the quick and I felt with renewed bitterness the injustices I had suffered. 'Enjoy recalling my childhood? Me? Every single room here reminds me of the terrible time I had and the way I was tortured.'

'You must be mad,' said Andrei indignantly. 'You were the most spoiled of all. Nobody tortured any of us.'

I looked at Nyuta, but she stayed with head bent over her plate and said nothing. Then I turned to Mother.

'But you used to beat me yourself, and wake me up at four in the morning to give me lessons and then pull my hair,' I said, looking fixedly at her. 'And Savelyev thrashed me with a rope and a whip and used to kick me with his boots and beat me with his clenched fists until my whole body was covered with bruises and weals. That's why Nyuta used to wash me herself, so that the servants wouldn't know what he had done to me.'

There was a moment's astonished silence before exclamations came from all sides. 'What nonsense! As if Mother and the rest of us wouldn't have known!'

'As if the serfs would not have said anything when they hated Savelyev so. . . .'

'This is completely fantastic,' said Mother with a shrug of her shoulders.

Furious that nobody would believe me, I obstinately went

on to tell them how I used to hide from Savelyev in the peasants' huts and had to jump into muddy ditches to avoid meeting him. 'Oh yes,' I finished up, 'I certainly experienced in my childhood the full force of Mother's care and affection!'

But then Sasha's eyes met mine and I realized from their silent reproach how wrong and cruel I had been to say what I had said at our first meeting after so long a separation. All the same, it was too late by then to put things right.

'Nyuta,' said Zarya, 'you're the best one to say whether or not there's any sense in all these ravings.'

'She is telling the truth.' Nyuta spoke softly without raising her head: then suddenly burst into tears and covered her face with a handkerchief.

'What . . . your husband was really cruel to her like that? And you knew about his appalling behaviour?' Mother cried, her face flaming with anger. 'You were never distinguished for intelligence, but at least you used to be honest with me. What made you keep these frightful happenings to yourself?'

'I suppose it was to improve my intelligence that you made me marry a lunatic.' Nyuta's eyes were dry now, and to get her own back on Mother she was trying to distil into her words all the malice that had accumulated in her heart. 'I admit I never told you what the husband you thrust upon me did to Liza. But you could have put two and two together. Don't you remember the weals and bruises you saw on my body the night he fired at me? You saw them, but as usual you forgot. What did your children ever mean to you? The estate always came first. Naturally I didn't want to tell you about the awful things he did: you would have thrown him out of your house and he would have dragged me with him, and then I would have been left alone with the brute. Of course I was wrong, but what about the way you behaved when . . .'

'That's enough!' my brothers cried. 'This is terrible. Nyuta, please be quiet at once.'

Everybody rose from the table.

'What have I done, what have I done?' I asked myself over and over again. And I took Sasha's hand and led her into the nursery. When we were alone there I pressed myself against her as I had done when I was a child. The tears were pouring from my eyes and I could not speak. As if she guessed my thoughts, she began to stroke my head.